How to Receive

DISCERNABLE ANSWERS

To Your Prayers

How to Receive DISCERNABLE ANSWERS To Your Prayers

Jeffrey R. Young

Second Printing: March 2005

International Standard Book Number:
0-88290-752-2

Horizon Publishers' Catalog and Order Number:
C2016

Printed and distributed
in the United States of America by

CEDAR FORT

& Distributors, Incorporated

Address:
925 North Main Street
Springville, Utah 84663

Local Phone: (801) 489-4084
Toll Free: 1 (800) SKYBOOK
FAX: (800) 489-1097

Contents

To My Wife—Joy

I will impart unto you of my Spirit, which shall enlighten your mind, which shall fill your soul with joy. (D&C 11:13)

Preface

The concept of receiving discernable answers to our prayers relentlessly occupied my mind and gently pressed upon my feelings for over a decade. Such relentless but gentle nudging by the Spirit motivated me to research and reduce to writing what I understand to be the process by which we can each learn to receive discernable answers to our prayers.

The effort to write this book caused me to reach several conclusions:

I wish I were as smart and insightful about the doctrine and practice of prayer as I thought I was when I began the effort.

Just because I have written this book does not mean that I can actually remember everything about that which I have written. I often use these materials as a resource myself.

Certain principles and doctrines are easier to write about than to practice.

I am in awe of the accomplished Latter-day Saint authors who have produced such researched, insightful and scholarly works without the benefit of word processors or the internet. I give my deepest thanks to the internet, its creators and operators.

Most of all, I have come to understand that there is a discernable answer to every prayer.

I sincerely hope that I used and interpreted the scriptures properly. If there has been any misinterpretation or misapplication of the scriptures, such misinterpretation or misapplication was not intended. At all times, I tried to understand, use and apply the scriptures within the bounds of their intended meanings and applications.

The words of others have added great strength to the contents of this book. In the course of writing, I would sometimes review old notes or drafts of the manuscript that contained a few sentences or word combinations that seemed extra special—as if they flowed from the doors of heaven.

There is a great need for personal revelation in our lives, in our families and in the church. I hope our application of the principles and practices delineated in this book will strengthen our capacity to pray, as well as our ability to recognize the answers to our prayers that will continue to come.

May each person that picks up this book find the reading enjoyable and the message clear. Likewise, may your prayers become mighty and your answers discernable.

—Jeffrey R. Young

1
Just One Question

The Question

It was instantaneous—a matter of seconds at most. In fact, it may have only been the lightning-fast thoughts of a daydream. The event occurred in the early summer of 1988, a summer filled with my relentless efforts to find full-time employment, something I had not had in eight months. It was about 8:15 in the morning on a bright, sunny day in Denver. The sunlight was shining through the window onto the bedroom floor. While putting the bedspread on the bed, I had a thought—perhaps an experience. In the space of a second or two, I imagined what I would say if a heavenly messenger appeared at my bedroom door, declaring that he would answer any one question I wanted to ask.

My first impulse was to ask, "Where can I go to find employment so that I can provide for my family?" I wanted a business name, address and contact person so that I could go to that address, and, with my resume in hand, declare, "Here I am, ready to go to work." I quickly concluded that knowing the answer to that question would be completely useless if, while traveling to my new job opportunity, I were hit by a bus and killed.

My next thought was to ask, "How long will I live?" I was thinking that knowing how long I had to live would help me know whether I was wasting my time even looking for work, especially if I were going to die within the very near future. Quickly, I concluded that this was not the question I wanted to ask.

Next, I considered asking, "If I were to die right now, which kingdom of glory would I be worthy to enter?" I thought that by receiving some sort of worthiness rating, I would know whether I should continue conducting myself and living my life as I had, or whether there were massive improvements or changes required if

I were to be worthy of exaltation after this life. My thoughts quickly processed that the answer to this question would be of great value to me in many ways; however, I would still be without the answer to my primary concern—"Where can I find a job?" Also, I thought that if the answer were provided, the answer would be of little substantive value if I had but a short time to live. If I were living a good life, but only had hours or minutes to live, I might have little or no time to share the good news with my family and encourage them to do likewise. Similarly, if my life needed a major course correction, but there was no time to repent and rebuild, what good would it do me to know to which kingdom of glory I was headed?

Then, into my mind burst the question I knew I would ask the heavenly messenger that was "standing" at my bedroom door: "How can I receive discernable answers to my prayers?" I knew this was the question for me to ask, because I knew that if I could learn to receive discernable answers to all of my prayers, I could eventually know what I must do in order to learn the answers to any other question I might want to ask.

During our mortal existence, we are granted the opportunity to learn how to recognize, then follow the various communications or "voices" used by the Father, Son and Holy Ghost. As we learn to recognize these divine "voices," we must also deal with the ongoing struggles of life, such as school work, relationships, the death of a loved one, physical limitations, lack of enthusiasm, pressure to succeed, church callings, parenting, running a business, finding employment, losing weight, finding a mate, or not having enough hours in a day. Keeping in mind that "it must needs be that there is an opposition in all things" (2 Nephi 2:11), we see that life's daily struggles do three things: *First,* they cause us to realize we need a power greater than ourselves, to help us when our abilities are not enough. *Second,* they motivate us to call upon that power through prayer. *Third,* they distract us from, and interfere with the very divine directives we seek. It is ironic that the "things" that stimulate someone to call upon God for his help are the very "things" that divert our attention from the answers he desires to give us. For example, a father's thoughts may be so focused on the unkind words last spoken to him by another family member that he cannot recognize the inspiration God has provided him in answer to his prayers for help with his church calling. When people do not recognize the answers to their prayers, it is easy for them to conclude that their prayers are not being heard or are not being answered.

Our Many Pleas

Millions, if not billions, of people since the time of Adam have at one time or another felt that their prayers, their pleas for help, their cries for relief or comfort, have gone unheard or unanswered. Feeling this way is not at all uncommon. Most likely, every reader of this book who has ever prayed has experienced similar feelings. This is easily illustrated by one of my wife's closest friends who sent an email message, commenting on her unanswered prayers. She wrote in an imploring tone, "Yesterday in Relief Society they talked about how mothers can get inspiration on what to do to help their kids. Why don't I feel that I get any?" Is the mother who asked this pleading question alone?

On the one hand, yes, she is alone in that she feels like no one hears her cries for help. Yes, she is alone, because it seems to her that she is not getting the divine help she wants and needs in rearing her children. On the other hand, no, she is not alone, because there are thousands, maybe millions of mothers who at this very moment feel just as alone and helpless as she does. And finally, no, she is not alone because God, her Heavenly Father, sees and hears her every prayer, thought and sigh of exasperation.

It is difficult to cope with such prayerful exasperation. Francine Bennion understands this frustration when she says,

> We all know people [who] testify that God answers their prayers, that they have received help on such matters as where to find a lost wallet, whom to marry, what occupation to choose, and how to teach children to keep clean rooms. They bear moving testimony of direct daily help in problem solving. Unless we are among that group so blessed, we may feel dismayed, frustrated, or even guilt-ridden by such assertions. However, when someone has prayed with all his soul and yet has sensed no guidance on important matters, he may feel that he lacks sufficient

faith, or that God chooses to give him no help, or that he can't help, or that he doesn't exist.[1]

When someone does not receive an answer to his or her prayers, why does it feel so frustrating? It is frustrating for two reasons: first, the person fully expects to receive an answer—there is a basic faith that an answer will come. Second, not getting an answer to a prayer does not feel right. In most instances the person seeking an answer does not have enough patience to go with their expectation that there will be an answer to their prayer. Most people find that waiting for the answer is like waiting for Christmas morning, hoping that the answer is in the first wrapped present that they open. Sometimes it is. Much of the time it is not. It is necessary to be patient and wait for the answer Heavenly Father is willing to provide, at the time he is willing to provide it. Notwithstanding our impatience, it is appropriate to expect and have faith that there will be an answer to every prayer. The scriptures teach that, "*Every one that asketh receiveth;* and he that seeketh findeth; and to him that knocketh it shall be opened." (Luke 11:10; Matthew 7:8)

When faith, hope, works and patience are present, an answer is expected. Sometimes the internal, spiritual barometer that everyone possesses tells us we ought to receive an answer, but our physical eyes, ears and heart have not yet perceived one. When this happens, it is understandable that one would feel like asking, "Does God love me less than those whose prayers he has answered? Am I smart enough not to need his help? Was my prayer even heard? Does he really care about me? Is Heavenly Father really there?"

Our Heavenly Father

Our Heavenly Father is there and he lives. As faithful people strive to receive and recognize answers to their prayers, it is important to have a general understanding of the divine being to whom we pray—God, Our Heavenly Father. Let us briefly focus on what is known about him as it relates to our prayers.

Foremost, he exists, he lives and he is a God who has a body, parts and passions. He has eyes to see us, ears to hear us, a mind to

1. Francine Bennion, "Stone or Bread?" *Ensign,* Jan. 1976, 38.

understand us, a heart to sense and feel every emotion anyone may experience, and a mouth to speak to us. As the father of our spirits, he wants to inspire us, reveal to us and answer us. This is exemplified in his appearance to the young boy, Joseph Smith. From Joseph Smith's experience comes additional knowledge and the witness that God is real, he knows our names, hears our prayers and communicates his will to those who pray with faith and sincerity. His ability and capacity to answer every prayer is beyond everyone's ability and capacity to comprehend how he does it. His capabilities are so great, that "it shall come to pass, that before they call, I will answer; and while they are yet speaking, I will hear." (Isaiah 65:24)

Heavenly Father is willing to do more than answer our prayers. He will go beyond the extra mile, by giving more than that for which someone has asked. The scriptures teach that, "If thou shalt ask, thou shalt receive revelation upon revelation, knowledge upon knowledge, that thou mayest know the mysteries and peaceable things—that which bringeth joy, that which bringeth life eternal." (D&C 42:61) The scriptures are filled with revelations men have received from God, plus, many references to other "things" that cannot be written at this time.[2]

It is known that God is a generous giver and that he may answer a prayer by providing much more than the simple answer that one seeks. It is also known that the heavens are open, and that Heavenly Father's revelation of his will to us is continuous. One of the Articles of Faith teaches this: "We believe all that God has revealed, all that He does now reveal, and we believe that He will yet reveal many great and important things pertaining to the Kingdom of God." (Article of Faith 9)

Prayer Works

Knowing that God will yet reveal many important things helps us realize that prayer is essential to salvation. Prayer is not a practice of small consequence, or an action we take when the notion strikes us.

---

2. Joseph Smith—History 1:20; 1 Nephi 9:1; 2 Nephi 33:1; Helaman 5:32-33; Words Of Mormon 1:5; 3 Nephi 17:15-17; 3 Nephi 19:32-34.

It is a divine decree of heaven, revealed in, and supported by, the scriptures. God's decree in the first dispensation was that everyone shall "Repent and call upon God in the name of the Son forevermore." Following this decree, "Adam and Eve, his wife, ceased not to call upon God." (Moses 5:8,16)

In Book of Mormon times, Christ specifically exhorted the Nephites at least ten times to "pray unto the Father in his name."[3] Both Nephi and Moroni taught the same principle.[4]

Today, the instruction is, "Ask, and ye shall receive; knock, and it shall be opened unto you." (D&C 4:7) Also, priesthood holders in the church are assigned to "visit the house of each member, and exhort them to pray vocally and in secret." (D&C 20:47)

The commandment to pray is not a hollow directive. There is a consequence when one is disobedient to this divine counsel. To the Latter-day Saints the Lord warns: "He that observeth not his prayers before the Lord in the season thereof, let him be had in remembrance before the judge of my people." (D&C 68:33) Another way to evaluate the importance of prayer is to look at an experience of the brother of Jared. On a very special occasion, the Lord talked with the brother of Jared for a period of three hours. Out of that three-hour visit with the Lord, the only topic that we know was discussed was prayer. Specifically, the brother of Jared was chastised because he had not remembered to pray.[5]

The commandment to pray is a commandment overflowing with blessings. Many of these blessings are identified directly in the scriptural verses where the very commandment is given. These blessings include:

- *Life for the soul.* "Incline your ear, and come unto me: hear, and your soul shall live." (Isaiah 55:3)
- *Receiving an abundance of the Spirit.* "Pray always, and I will pour out my Spirit upon you, and great shall be your bless-

3. 3 Nephi 13:6-9; 17:3; 18:19-21, 23, 30; 20:31; 21:27; 27:2-7, 9, 28.
4. 1 Nephi 7:21; 2 Nephi 32:9; Moroni 8:3.
5. Ether 2:14.

ing—yea, even more than if you should obtain treasures of earth and corruptibleness to the extent thereof." (D&C 19:38)

- *Being directed.* "Counsel with the Lord in all thy doings, and he will direct thee for good; yea, when thou liest down at night lie down unto the Lord, that he may watch over you in your sleep; and when thou risest in the morning let thy heart be full of thanks unto God; and if ye do these things, ye shall be lifted up at the last day." (Alma 37:37)
- *Avoiding Temptation.* "Behold, verily, verily, I say unto you, ye must watch and pray always lest ye enter into temptation." (3 Nephi 18:15, 18)
- *Families being blessed.* "Pray in your families unto the Father, always in my name, that your wives and your children may be blessed." (3 Nephi 18:21)
- *Never being alone.* "Praying always that they faint not; and inasmuch as they do this, I will be with them even unto the end." (D&C 75:11)

It is motivating and comforting to know that there are specific blessings provided when we obey the Lord's commandment to pray. While there may be additional blessings that come from obedience to this commandment, these six are marvelous.

An Answer for Every Prayer

This spiritual reality must be declared: there is an answer to every sincere prayer. Everyone that asks receives an answer.[6] Even though there is an answer to every prayer, almost everyone has had the experience of offering a prayer that he or she believes was not answered. Having such an experience is generally very frustrating, especially to the men and women who felt that they were doing their best to keep the commandments, to fulfill their church callings and to be the best person they could possibly be. For some of them, the frustration was probably so great that it may have caused them to actually cry out, "Why can't I get an answer?"

Coping with the erroneous notion that a prayer was not answered would be much less frustrating if members of the church had been

6. Luke 11:10.

taught in the scriptures that only 50 or 60 percent of their prayers would ever be answered. That way, whenever someone felt a prayer was not answered, he could resignedly conclude, "I guess this must be one of those times when there is no answer to my prayer." Gratefully, that is not the case. There is always an answer to every prayer! Just because a person may not have understood, discerned or otherwise perceived the answer given, does not mean an answer was not provided.

Whenever believing people feel that they have not been given an answer to their prayers, it may simply be a symptom that they were lacking in faith, dealing with worthiness issues, asking for something that was not right, or were unwilling to wait patiently for the answer.[7] It may also be that they suffered only from an underdeveloped ability to recognize the answer that was, in fact, provided. Whatever the reason, their failure to recognize the answer shows that they most likely needed to develop a more Christ-like character, prepare differently for their prayers, learn how to pray properly, or they needed to learn how to recognize the various means by which the answer could have been revealed.

As one can see, there are many reasons that explain why someone may feel a prayer may not have been answered. These various reasons will be discussed in the following chapters of the book. First, it must be reemphasized that there *is* an answer for every prayer. This point must be stressed in the hope that everyone will keep two other important considerations in mind: (1) One of our earthly purposes is to learn to make our own decisions so that we can gain knowledge and grow from the consequences of those decisions. (2) No one should feel that any matters in life are so trivial and of such small consequence that they do not merit either a prayer or an answer.

Even though there are no matters in life too small or trivial about which we can pray, it should not be suggested that anyone should spend time praying for direction on matters that the individual ought to decide for him or herself.

---

7. Alma 10:6.

There is a story about a young woman who bore her testimony in church, during which she highlighted the spirituality of her husband. She was impressed that while shopping together, he would not even choose between various brands of canned beans without first praying about which brand he should select. Offering a prayer under such circumstances may strike some people as inappropriate. Years ago, I would have wholeheartedly agreed. Even though I still feel somewhat that way today, it is inappropriate to make a blanket statement that some matters are too trivial to pray about.

When that young husband prayed about which brand of canned beans to select, God's answer to *that* husband's prayer might have been: (1) "Young man, it is not necessary for *you* to pray about which brand of canned vegetables *you* should buy." (2) "Make your own decision." (3) "It does not matter to me, one way or the other."[8] One can even imagine God answering, "Young man, that is a trivial matter. *You* do not need to trouble me with such unimportant matters." What is unimaginable is God not answering that prayer simply because the subject matter was supposedly "trivial." Additionally, when Heavenly Father tells that young husband that *he* does not need to pray about brands of canned vegetables, Heavenly Father is not telling all people that they should not pray about what brands of vegetables they should purchase. What Heavenly Father may deem to be a trivial matter for one person, he may not deem to be a trivial matter for another.

Here are some questions to think about. Is it trivial to pray about what brand of pain reliever to buy? Is it inappropriate to ask God whether the vehicle one is about to purchase is the right one for his or her family? Is it trivial to pray about which airline flight to take? It should be obvious that the answer to all three questions is a resounding NO!

Such prayers are not at all trivial. Remember the time when pain relief capsules on drugstore shelves were maliciously laced with cyanide? Such prayers are not trivial when a man considers that he could have purchased a particular automobile that came equipped with defective tires, resulting in rollover accidents. Such prayers are

---

8. D&C 80:3. See also D&C 60:5; 61:22; 62:5.

not trivial when a woman could have booked a reservation on an airline flight that crashed into the World Trade Center. What one person considers a trivial matter, another person may consider a choice between life and death. Unless it is revealed to you otherwise, there are no trivial prayers.

Do you sense the significance of what is being taught? Without intending to be irreverent by putting words in Heavenly Father's mouth, it should be easy for everyone to imagine Heavenly Father giving the following counsel: "I will always provide an answer to your prayers; however, from time-to-time, that answer will be, 'It does not matter to me what you decide or choose to do—whatever decision or choice you make is acceptable to me and is not contrary to my will for you. I have heard and answered every prayer you have ever offered and I will hear and answer every prayer you will yet offer.'"[9]

Unless it is revealed to someone otherwise, all prayers about "trivial" matters should not automatically be labeled inappropriate or a misuse of spiritual resources. If a child were hungry and asked for a slice of bread, would you satisfy her hunger by giving her a stone? If a child were to ask for an apple, would you satisfy her request by giving her a rattlesnake? If a child were to ask for a hard-boiled egg, would you give her a scorpion? No, of course not. No father or mother who loves his or her child would attempt to satisfy that need in such a hurtful manner. In a wonderful section of scripture on prayer, it is abundantly clear that if loving, mortal and imperfect parents know how to satisfy the sincere entreaties of their children, then everyone should know how much more our Heavenly Father shall give to those that ask of him.[10]

Our Heavenly Father is not a giver of stones, serpents or scorpions. He is always a giver of the Spirit, truth and light. Consequently, if everyone is to fulfill their personal revelation expectations and

---

9. Former U.S. President Jimmy Carter once stated on "Larry King Live," CNN TV, "God answers all the prayers. Sometimes he answers 'Yes,' sometimes he answers 'No,' and sometimes the answer is, 'You gotta be kidding.'"

10. Luke 11:11-14; 3 Nephi 14:9-11.

receive understandable answers to their prayers, it is their responsibility to (1) Acquire the characteristics of a seeker of truth and light, (2) Prepare for prayer, (3) Pray properly, and (4) Recognize personal revelation when it is given. As individuals expand their abilities in these four areas, they will receive discernable answers to their prayers—answers that they recognize as specific, personal, revelation.

2
The Seeker of Truth and Light

Character Traits

The principles have been established that prayer is essential to salvation, that God hears every prayer, that prayer works, and that there is an answer for every prayer. The acknowledgment of these truths, coupled with a sincere desire and expectation that an answer to our prayers will be provided, requires the fulfillment of certain responsibilities as prerequisites to receiving that answer. The main responsibility of every man and woman is to be worthy of the divine revelation that he or she seeks. This implies that when someone asks for help with a particular virtue or for a particular blessing, then he or she should work diligently for that blessing and cultivate that virtue.[1] While some prayers may be answered notwithstanding one's condition of worthiness or unworthiness, some prayers will not be answered unless they are received the old-fashioned way. They must be earned.

Whatever the answer one hopes to receive or whatever the answer God chooses to provide, in almost everyone's heart of hearts, it is the Lord's will that everyone wants to be done. Heavenly Father's revealed will is his word, his truth.[2] To merit such answers to our prayers, it is necessary that each of us acquire the temperament and character of a seeker of truth and light—we must strive to develop a character that is as Christ-like as possible.

With this in mind, there are a couple of character traits everyone must strive to avoid. These two objectionable traits will be identified and discussed, followed by an examination of several character traits almost everyone will want to develop:

---

1. Ezra Taft Benson, "Pray Always," *Ensign,* Feb. 1990, 4.
2. D&C 84:45.

Character Traits Everyone Will Want to Eliminate

1. **Hard-heartedness.**

Prayers are much more likely to be answered for those whose hearts are softened. This point is explained very well by Chauncey C. Riddle:

> The first intimations of revelation from the Holy Spirit are feelings in our heart—feelings of good and bad, feelings of sympathy for suffering, feelings of longing for spiritual insight. To ignore or to quash these feelings is hard-heartedness. Those who demand that everything be decided in terms of physical things are thus hard-hearted. They cannot learn to pray and to be guided by the Holy Spirit because they reject it when it tries to get through to them."[3]

If one avoids hard-heartedness by becoming loving and charitable, one becomes open to the promptings of the Spirit. This results in receiving an understanding of those matters that are generally hard to understand.[4]

2. **Selfishness.**

Perhaps the best account depicting this bad example is the tale of King Noah in the Book of Mormon. King Noah was taught at the feet of a father who loved God and people more than material possessions. Notwithstanding such an upbringing, King Noah sought only pleasure and the enjoyment of material things, and he sought these pleasures and comforts of life at the expense of others. To accomplish his selfish ends, King Noah abandoned the teachings of his father, employing tyrannical means and methods. King Noah did not work to support himself, but rather taxed the people one-fifth of all their possessions to construct elegant buildings for himself, his wives and many concubines. As Chauncey C. Riddle puts it,

---

3. Chauncey C. Riddle, "Obstacles to Prayer," *Ensign,* Jan. 1976, 27.

4. 1 Ne. 15:3, 8, 11; Jarom 1:4.

People who overvalue the things of the physical order have to have more and more goods and pleasures to stay satisfied. This kind of appetite cannot be satisfied except through oppression: getting someone else to do the work to provide material abundance. It is a curious paradox that people who live for material pleasures generally detest work and try to find a slave to do it for them, whereas people who treasure the things of the Spirit learn to love work and they work hard to produce material blessings for others. The point of all this is that selfishness and glorying in carnal security cut one off from the Holy Spirit so that he cannot pray effectively. True prayer leads to righteousness; but righteousness is achieved only in sacrifice. The last thing the selfish person wants is sacrifice, so he naturally does not pray very successfully."[5]

Character Traits Every Seeker of Truth Will Want to Develop

1. **The Ability to Listen.**

The ability to listen is an attribute that serves everyone well in day-to-day relationships, whether at home, school or the workplace. That ability is equally as important in the relationship we have with our Heavenly Father. President Spencer W. Kimball offered this counsel,

> Your prayers ought to include some intense listening. When we pray, do we just speak, or do we also listen? Our Savior . . . stands and knocks. If we do not listen, He will not sup with us nor give answer to our prayers. We must learn how to listen, grasp, interpret, understand. The Lord stands knocking. He never retreats. But He will never force Himself upon us. If our distance from Him increases, it is we who have moved and not the Lord. And should we ever fail to get an answer to our prayers, we must look into our own lives for a reason."[6]

---

5. Chauncey C. Riddle, "Obstacles to Prayer," *Ensign,* Jan. 1976, 27.
6. Spencer W. Kimball, *Faith Precedes the Miracle,* Salt Lake City: Deseret Book Company. 1972, 208.

2. **Faith.**

We have been taught in the scriptures that without faith, we can do nothing; therefore, we must ask in faith.[7] We must have faith that our prayers will be both heard and answered. If we pray for the right things to the Father in the name of the Son, our prayers will be answered.[8] If we pray with exceeding faith, we will be consoled in our afflictions and the Lord will send down justice upon those who seek to destroy us.[9] When we trust in the Lord's Spirit, our minds will be enlightened and our souls will be filled with joy.[10] As we exercise faith when we pray, we take ourselves one step closer to understanding the mysteries of God.[11] This is because the prayers of the faithful shall be heard.[12]

3. **Honesty.**

Perhaps the single greatest virtue one can possess is an honest character. To be honest in thought, purpose and action will draw an individual closer to true communication with God than any other character trait. If honesty is lacking in the individual offering a prayer, there will be a conflict, however subtle, in the channels of communication. Since truth never conflicts with truth, when there is a lack of truth or honesty, there is always a conflict. Honesty in the divine process of prayer eliminates the conflict and cleanses the communication.

4. **Humility.**

Humility in prayer brings great blessings. The Old Testament scriptures tell us that, "If my people, which are called by my name, shall humble themselves, and pray, and seek my face, and turn from their wicked ways; then will I hear from heaven, and will forgive their sin, and will heal their land." (2 Chronicles 7:14.) Modern-day scriptures teach us that, "A man may have

---

7. D&C 8:10; See also 3 Ne. 18:20.
8. 3 Ne. 18:20.
9. Jacob 3:1.
10. D&C 11:12-14.
11. Alma 26:22.
12. 2 Ne. 26:15.

many revelations, and have power to do many mighty works, yet if he boasts in his own strength, and sets at naught the counsels of God, and follows after the dictates of his own will and carnal desires, he must fall and incur the vengeance of a just God upon him." (D&C 3:4.) It is imperative, if for no other reason than to hold on to blessings already given, that men and women be humble even when they are intelligent, well-educated, good-looking or wealthy; however, if they allow themselves to become prideful or puffed up because of their intelligence, education, good looks or wealth, the door of prayer on which they knock will not be opened to them.[13] As Oliver Cowdery once noted, "The Lord . . . is rich in mercy, and ever willing to answer the consistent prayer of the humble. . . ."[14]

One of the exceedingly great blessings that comes from being humble is the promise in Doctrine and Covenants 112:10, that the Lord will lead us by the hand and give us answers to our prayers.

5. **Integrity.**

Integrity is inseparably connected to honesty. Integrity is the action part of an honest character. The actions of a man or woman of integrity will be congruent with the thoughts of his or her heart as well as the mind and will of the Lord. Bruce R. McConkie ties these two character traits together very well. He says it this way,

> Our deeds, in large measure, are children of our prayers. Having prayed, we act; our proper petitions have the effect of charting a righteous course of conduct for us. The boy that prays (earnestly and devoutly and in faith) that he may go on a mission, will then prepare himself for his mission, and in fact receives his call to service. The young people who pray always, in faith, to marry in the temple, and then act accordingly, are never satisfied with worldly marriage. So intertwined are prayer and works that having recited the law of prayer in detail, Amulek then concludes: 'After ye have done all these things, if ye turn

---

13. 2 Ne. 9:42.
14. Oliver Cowdery's endnote, Joseph Smith—History; See also D&C 1:28.

> away the needy, and the naked, and visit not the sick and afflicted, and impart of your substance, if ye have, to those who stand in need—I say unto you, if ye do not any of these things, behold, your prayer is vain, and availeth you nothing, and ye are as hypocrites who do deny the faith.'(Alma 34:28)"[15]

In summary, Joseph Smith stated it succinctly, "Be men of integrity and truth."[16]

6. **Obedience.**

A person who has made a personal and long-term commitment to live his life in a manner consistent with God's teachings and commandments, and is acting in accordance with that commitment, is obedient. Chauncey C. Riddle discusses obedience as he talks about a time of great distress and trial for the house of Israel. The Lord had chosen Saul, of the tribe of Benjamin, to be their king. He observes,

> Anointed under the hand of Samuel, the prophet, Saul also received instruction from the Lord through Samuel. In his obedience he had great success. But then he grew great in his own sight and felt he no longer needed to obey. During this time, the Lord instructed Saul to go to Amalek and utterly destroy it because of their persistent wickedness, slaying "man and woman, infant and suckling, ox and sheep, camel and ass." (1 Sam. 15:1-5.) Saul's obedience was only partial, was self-serving: he spared Agag, king of the Amalekites, and the best of the Amalekite sheep and oxen. When Samuel discovered this, Saul rationalized that the livestock were to be used for sacrifice for the Lord. "And Samuel said, Hath the Lord as great delight in burnt offerings and sacrifices, as in obeying the voice of the Lord? Behold, to obey is better than sacrifice, and to hearken than the fat of rams. For rebellion is as the

15. Bruce R. McConkie, "Why the Lord Ordained Prayer," *Ensign,* Jan.1976, 7.

16. *Encyclopedia of Joseph Smith's Teachings,* edited by Larry E. Dahl and Donald Q. Cannon, Salt Lake City: Bookcraft, Inc., 1997, 338.

> sin of witchcraft, and stubbornness is as iniquity and idolatry. Because thou hast rejected the word of the Lord, he hath also rejected thee from being king. . . . And as Samuel turned about to go away, [Saul] laid hold upon the skirt of his mantle, and it rent. And Samuel said unto him, The Lord hath rent the kingdom of Israel from thee this day, and hath given it to a neighbour of thine, that is better than thou." (1 Sam. 15:22-23, 27-28.)
>
> The story of King Saul stands as a solemn warning to all of us. If the time ever comes that we think we can better serve God by following our own wisdom than we can by following the direction of the Lord through his Holy Spirit and through his holy prophets, we have apostatized. If we thus reject the Lord, we have broken the slender thread of communication. Our prayers cannot then be effective. We might speculate as to what caused King Saul to disobey. Was it pride? Was it fear of the people? Was it carelessness or thoughtlessness? Whatever the cause the result was the same: Saul no longer feared God. The purpose of prayer is to gain the knowledge and strength to do the will of God. Disobedience makes of prayer a mockery in us, even as it did for Saul.[17]

7. **A Teachable Nature.**

Those who possess a teachable nature are willing to be enlightened, instructed or trained. Such a characteristic is distinguishable from humility. One who is humble will almost always be teachable; however, one who is teachable will not necessarily be humble. Arthur R. Bassett addresses this character trait:

> It seems to me that we need to go to prayer with a more open attitude—as nearly as this is possible—with a more sincere desire to be taught. Perhaps our sole petition initially should be that he will teach us what we ought to pray for. This is in effect a request that he will inspire us concerning the questions we should ask, the problems we should pose for him in prayer. We are told that when the

17. Chauncey C. Riddle, "Obstacles to Prayer," *Ensign,* Jan. 1976, 27; See also D&C 46:7-9.

> Savior was among the Nephites and they entered into prayer with him that "they did . . . continue, without ceasing, to pray unto him; and they did not multiply many words, for it was given unto them what they should pray, and they were filled with desire." (3 Ne. 19:24.)[18]

Those who are teachable will yield to the Lord's agenda for their life rather than persisting, or insisting, on following their own.

8. **Personal Righteousness.**

Revelation is for everyone, not just for a select few who find themselves serving in positions of perceived importance in the church. Neither one's current church position nor one's past church service qualify an individual for, or confer upon such an individual, any special rights to revelation or inspiration that are unavailable to anyone else. Church position does not confer spiritual gifts. Bishops, stake presidents and apostles each hold a calling to serve. Every calling to serve is a calling to repent, a calling to become more righteous. It is personal righteousness, not a calling to a particular church office, that will open the windows of revelation to a seeker of truth.

Thomas S. Monson has taught us,

> The greatest force in this world today is the power of God as it works through man. If we are on the Lord's errand, we are entitled to the Lord's help. That divine help, however, is predicated upon our worthiness. To sail safely the seas of mortality, to perform a human rescue mission, we need the guidance of that eternal mariner—even the great Jehovah. We reach out, we reach up, to obtain heavenly help.[19]

9. **A Willingness to Ponder the Scriptures.**

Pondering is not a leisure activity—it requires an intense mental participation. As we ponder the scriptures (including our Patriarchal Blessings), we put ourselves in a position to be caught

---

18. Arthur R. Bassett, "Before Praying," *Ensign,* Jan. 1976, 31.

19. Thomas S. Monson, "Your Eternal Voyage," *Ensign,* May 2000, 46; See also Alma 5:57.

away in the Spirit of the Lord where truths can be revealed.[20] Pondering demands that we think, think harder, and then think some more, in order that we might find meanings, interpretations and impressions that will help us understand a matter or make a decision. Joseph Smith provides an excellent example of pondering the scriptures. After reading James 1:5, Joseph reflected on that verse again and again. It was only after pondering that scripture at length that he was able to come to a conclusion as to what he had to do.[21] Pondering enables us to think and understand in Christ-like ways. Such a combined mental and spiritual effort may also result in the enlightening of our minds.[22]

10. **An Attitude of Emulating the Savior.**

The Savior is our exemplar. "Every seeker after truth should searchingly and honestly ask himself or herself this question: Am I attempting to climb heavenward by some other path than the one charted by my Savior and Redeemer?" As various choices or actions are considered, a popular question is always worth asking before a decision is made, "What would Jesus do?"

11. **Sincerity (Real Intent).**

We need to pray honestly and be willing to follow the will of the Father with our whole heart, without hypocrisy or deception in our thoughts or actions.[23] Moroni's words best explain the reason for praying to God with sincerity of heart: "And when ye shall receive these things, I would exhort you that ye would ask God, the Eternal Father, in the name of Christ, if these things are not true; and if ye shall ask with a sincere heart, with real intent, having faith in Christ, he will manifest the truth of it unto you, by the power of the Holy Ghost. And by the power of the Holy Ghost ye may know the truth of all things." (Moroni 10:4-5.) Is there anything that a seeker of truth requires from God in answer to a specific prayer, other than the manifestation of God's truth

---

20. 1 Ne. 11:1.
21. Joseph Smith—History 1:11-13.
22. D&C 138:11.
23. See 2 Nephi 31:13.

regarding such a matter? No, the seeker of truth requires only the word or will of the Lord.

12. **Being Open to Conviction.**

Following his death, Joseph Smith appeared to Brigham Young in a dream and instructed him as follows:

> Tell the people to be humble and faithful and be sure to keep the Spirit of the Lord and it will lead them right. Be careful and not turn away the still small voice; it will teach you what to do and where to go; it will yield the fruits of the kingdom. Tell the brethren to keep their hearts open to conviction, so that when the Holy Ghost comes to them, their hearts will be ready to receive it. They can tell the Spirit of the Lord from all other spirits—it will whisper peace and joy to their souls; it will take malice, hatred, strife and all evil from their hearts; and their whole desire will be to do good, bring forth righteousness and build up the kingdom of God."[24]

One whose heart is open to conviction is ready to receive revelation when it comes.

13. **Forgiveness.**

Members of the church are expected to be a forgiving people. A person unwilling to forgive cannot be protected from the feelings of resentment, jealousy, envy, hate or fear that can daily infect the soul. In New Testament times, Mark instructed: "And when ye stand praying, forgive, if ye have ought against any: that your Father also which is in heaven may forgive you your trespasses." (Mark 11:25.) Prayer always offers an opportunity to forgive someone toward whom we may have any unkind feelings. Without forgiving others, the harboring of such unkind feelings toward them will contribute to the withdrawal of the Spirit we are praying to attract.

14. **Repentant Attitude.**

A repentant person's prayer will be heard. Repentance results in meekness and lowliness of heart that pave the way for the

---

24. *Juvenile Instructor,* Jul. 1873, 114.

visitation of the Holy Ghost.[25] On the other hand, it is known from the scriptures that the prayer of the unrepentant may not be heard. "Except they repent . . . and cry mightily to the Lord their God, I will not hear their prayers" (Mosiah 11:25). The Lord's answer to an unrepentant person's prayer may very simply be this, "This is my answer to your prayers: I will not hear your prayers or provide another answer to your prayers until you repent."

15. **Reverence.**

Reverence beckons revelation. Consequently, we are constantly being reminded by our leaders to improve the reverence in our meetings, especially when we are in our chapels. Just as reverence summons revelation, irreverence impedes revelation. For that purpose, said President Boyd K. packer, "foyers are built into our chapels to allow for the greeting and chatter that are typical of people who love one another. However, when we step into the chapel, we must!—each of us must—watch ourselves lest we be guilty of intruding when someone is struggling to feel delicate spiritual communications."[26]

16. **Willingness to Fast.**

The practice of fasting is closely linked to effective prayer. Arthur R. Bassett describes the connection this way:

> When a person fasts he begins to draw his energies more completely from the inside than from the out. He symbolically turns his back on the things of the world in his hungering and thirsting after righteousness. In his quest for spiritual nourishment, he turns to Christ as the bread of life and the source of living water. As the hours and sometimes days of fasting begin to mount, a minor crisis is created in his life as he begins to sense more intensely the pangs of hunger. To over dramatize for purposes of emphasis, he finds himself caught, as it were, in a struggle

---

25. Moroni 8:26, Alma 22:16.

26. Boyd K Packer, *General Conference Report,* "Reverence Invites Revelation," *Ensign,* Nov. 1991, 22.

> between impending starvation and the establishment of contact with God. Fasting helps release us somewhat from this world. It helps us to recognize our dependence upon the Lord. It helps demonstrate the seriousness of our intent, both to ourselves and to the Lord. It is a first step in subjecting our will to his. Properly entered into, fasting helps increase our powers of concentration by impressing upon us the urgency of our quest. It is often an indispensable companion to effective prayer.[27]

The companionship between fasting and prayer is very effective. This companionship leads to greater humility and firmer faith, that together result in our being filled with joy.[28]

None of the sixteen Christ-like characteristics that have been discussed are sufficient by themselves. The need for development of each characteristic and its relationship to prayer varies with each person. Applying each characteristic to prayer in concert with the other characteristics will be a function of one's temperament, circumstances and life's day-to-day concerns.

The complexity of developing and adopting all of these characteristics as a part of our personality and applying them to prayer was effectively described by Neal A. Maxwell when he likened them to the tumblers on a combination lock:

> Petitioning in prayer has taught me, again and again, that the vault of heaven with all its blessings is to be opened only by a combination lock. One tumbler falls when there is faith; a second when there is personal righteousness; the third and final tumbler falls only when what is sought is, in God's judgment—not ours—right for us."[29]

---

27. Arthur R. Bassett, "Before Praying," *Ensign,* Jan. 1976, 31. See also Alma 5:45-46, Alma 17:3.

28. Helaman 3:35.

29. Neal A. Maxwell, "Insights," *New Era,* Apr. 1978, 6.

No matter how long or hard we pound on the vault door, our access to the treasures of heaven will not occur without the spiritual tumblers falling properly into place.[30]

There may be other character traits that everyone would do well to cultivate. Everyone is encouraged to do so. When these Christ-like attributes and characteristics are adopted, people become continual seekers of truth and light—continual seekers of the Lord's will. The fruits of such attributes are a Christ-like character, a character that is worthy to open the vault door and receive the divine revelations that are sought in answer to prayers. With a more Christ-like disposition, one can have deeper relationships with family members and friends as well as with our Heavenly Father. It is not necessary to master all of these attributes in order to communicate with Heavenly Father. However, when we do, we are better prepared to receive discernable answers to our prayers.

---

30. "If you seek His help, be sure your life is clean, your motives are worthy, and you're willing to do what he asks—for He will Answer your prayers." Richard G. Scott, General Conference Report, "Learning to Recognize Answers to Prayer," *Ensign,* Nov. 1989, 32.

3
Preparations for Prayer

Proper Preparation

Proper preparation for prayer stimulates everyone to live the most Christ-like life he or she possibly can. Such preparation enables each person to know what to pray for, how to pray, and how to be prepared for the answer when it is provided—in no matter which of its many forms the answer may come. The preparations that can be made seem endless, perhaps because there seems to be an endless number of "things" in life that everyone feels he ought to be doing differently or better. At times such an effort may seem greater than one's ability to perform the task. Yet, step-by-step, as individuals become more Christ-like, they begin to prepare for prayer in their own unique ways.

Just as the process of preparation for prayer will be different for everyone, identical preparation by two individuals will produce different answers or results. Preparing for prayer is a complex process. Likewise, the application of the identical preparation process by the same person will produce similar results each time. Every person's unique character traits, as a seeker of the Lord's will, will result in divine inspiration, direction and revelation, tailor-made to each person's needs, desires and circumstances as God, in his infinite love, mercy and wisdom, sees fit.

Every sincere prayer that is offered is unique in its timing and circumstances. Consequently, it is important to keep in mind that we do not need to prepare for every prayer in the same manner each time. In fact, the activities of any given day assure that everyone will engage in a variety of preparation methods prior to whatever prayers may be offered. Since everybody's circumstances and time in mortality are constantly changing, each person is always relating to

Heavenly Father on a uniquely personal basis.[1] Most people are familiar with the expression that the key to the ninety-and-nine is the one. In our personal prayers, our Heavenly Father relates to each of us personally as if we were "the one."

The goal in one's preparations for prayer is to implement good practices that can be used to help attain a state of mind conducive to recognizing the promptings of the Spirit. It is not the suggestion that one engage in ritualistic practices, but rather that one should adopt preparations that will regularly contribute to achieving a state of spiritual readiness. There will always be unexpected changes in one's day that will affect his or her preparations; nevertheless, if there is a solid foundation to the preparation, one will be blessed as he or she prays for discernable answers to those prayers. Beyond adopting the character traits of a seeker of God's will, there are several other things one can do: (1) One can seek the Lord early. (2) One can pray in a setting of quietude. (3) One can pray in secret. (4) One can pray always.

Seek the Lord Early

Is there a better time of the day to offer a prayer? The bedrock answer to that question is "No," because there is no better time to pray than the moment at which one has the thought about praying. While there may be no time like the present, for a prayer, there are indications in the scriptures that the "early bird" may get the worm. The scriptures provide us with examples by Abraham, Moses, Joseph Smith and Jesus, each praying in the early part of the day. Here are applicable verses:

Abraham: "And Abraham gat up early in the morning to the place where he stood before the LORD." (Genesis 19:27) ***Moses:*** "And in the morning, then ye shall see the glory of the LORD." (Exodus 16:7) "And they rose up early in the morning, and gat them up into the top of the mountain, saying, Lo, we [be here], and will go up unto the place which the LORD hath promised: for we have sinned." (Numbers 14:40) ***Jesus:*** "And in the morning, rising up a great while before day, he went out and departed into a solitary

1. Matthew 18:12-14.

place, and there prayed." (Mark 1:35) ***Joseph Smith:*** "It was on the morning of a beautiful, clear day . . ." (Joseph Smith—History 1:14)

There is a great deal of value in arising early to pray. Early in the day the mind and body are fresh, alert and invigorated. That may be why the modern scriptures teach the church members to "Retire to thy bed early, that ye may not be weary; arise early, that your bodies and your minds may be invigorated." (D&C 88:124) Receiving discernable answers to prayers requires both a mental and physical effort. Certainly, praying at a time of day when the mind and body are at their peak enhances one's ability to hear the whisperings and feel the impressions of the Spirit. After all, "It was *on the morning* of a beautiful, clear day . . ." when Joseph Smith encountered the Father and the Son. (Joseph Smith—History 1:14)

Perhaps rather than emphasizing the time of day that a prayer is offered, it is more important that we call upon God early, meaning first, soon, or before it is "too late," for reasons both obvious and unknown. The scriptures provide us with many examples of praying sooner rather than later:

"I love them that love me; and those that seek me early shall find me." (Proverbs 8:17) "And again, be patient in tribulation until I come; and, behold, I come quickly, and my reward is with me, and they who have sought me early shall find rest to their souls." (D&C 54:10) "He that seeketh me early shall find me, and shall not be forsaken." (D&C 88:83)

One of the ways that everyone can prepare for prayer is by praying always. By praying continually, many will find that they will always be praying early—both early in the day as a first thought[2] and before it is "too late."

Quietude

Do people ever really notice how much noise there is around them? Everyone should stop, right now, and listen. What external noises can be heard? Because of the variety of noises that constantly fill the air, people do not hear everything they are capable of hearing. This is not because they are hard of hearing. It is because there

2. Romans 12:12.

is simply too much noise. Turn down the stereo and one can hear the TV. Now turn off the TV and one can hear the hum of the nearby computer. Turn off the computer and one can then hear the movement of the air through the heating vent. Turn off the airflow and one will hear an airplane flying high overhead. Every time a noise is eliminated, one can hear a quieter sound previously masked by the other sounds. The more noises that a person can eliminate, the easier it will be to hear that voice which is still and small.

There are also internal "noises" that interfere with the quietude we seek—noises such as pride, sin, impatience, contention, fatigue, stress, and irreverence. One will also discover that some noises are simultaneously external and internal. These noises such as music containing crude or offensive lyrics, television containing vulgar programming, movies containing lewd or suggestive scenes, and reading material containing obscene or distasteful contents—are such that they literally obstruct one or more of a person's senses and canker that person's sensitivity to the whisperings of the Spirit.

Why is quietude so important? It is important because inspiration and revelation will come to us more easily in peaceful settings.[3] This is not a suggestion that we must always find a place where we can pray in total silence. It is a suggestion that everyone should strive to eliminate those noises that obstruct their spiritual communications. Sometimes listening to beautiful music will repel many distracting noises while simultaneously contributing to an atmosphere that invites personal revelation. The basic principle of quietude is that if the Lord's voice is still and small, we, too, must be still.[4]

The world watched as the United States went into battle against its enemies in Operation Desert Storm in Kuwait and Iraq, and in Operation Enduring Freedom in Afghanistan. At the outset of each of these military efforts, the primary objective of the U.S. military was to interfere with and destroy the enemy's channels of communication. When such communication is destroyed, the enemy loses its command, control and communication capabilities, leaving its

---

3. Boyd K. Packer, *General Conference Report,* "Reverence Invites Revelation," *Ensign,* Nov. 1991, 21.

4. D&C 101:16; D&C 123:17.

entire military in disarray. The soldiers in the trenches do not know what to do or where to go. They receive no warnings of pending attacks or strategic directions on how to best defend themselves or whether or not to counterattack. When communication links are interrupted, the very life of every soldier is placed at the mercy of the relentless attacking forces.

That is exactly what Satan, the great adversary, tries to do to everyone. He is at war with every man and woman and will use any and all overt or cunning "noises" to interfere with or thwart the channels of communication with Heavenly Father.

Finding reverential quietude is a tough assignment. Even when we strive to eliminate the various noises that interfere with the quiet we need, there are times when our own, well-intentioned, purposeful activities adversely affect the quietude necessary for revelation. This point is well illustrated in the following story by Arthur Bassett:

> As a young seminary teacher I was impressed by some counsel from Elder Harold B. Lee, then a member of the Council of the Twelve, given to a group of seminary and institute instructors. A few weeks prior to our visit by Elder Lee, President David O. McKay had been reminding the Twelve of the necessity of being responsive to the whisperings of the Spirit. These promptings, he advised them, come when one is relaxed and not under the pressure of appointments. President McKay then took the occasion to relate to the Twelve an experience of one of the former General Authorities of the Church.
>
> The individual concerned had had a son who had been run over by a freight train. The boy's mother was inconsolable. She mourned during the three days prior to the funeral, received no comfort at the funeral, and was in a rather serious state of mind. One day soon after the funeral services, while she was lying on her bed relaxed but still mourning, she says that her son appeared to her and told her not to grieve. He reported to her that his death had been an accident. Then he reported—and this is the point Elder Lee wanted to make—that as soon as he realized that he was in another environment he tried to see his father, but couldn't reach him. His father was so busy with the duties of his office he could not respond to his call. Therefore, he had come to the

mother. He said to her, "You tell father that all is well with me, and I want you not to mourn anymore."

I knew immediately what Elder Lee was telling us. I was, at the time, a young seminary teacher beginning my teaching career, eager to do well in my newly chosen vocation and eager to please the Lord. I had been given a calling at the stake level as well as one in my own ward, in addition to my home teaching assignment. Being relatively new in the community I was accepting a speaking engagement nearly every Sunday evening. All of this was in addition to everything I was trying to do in developing lesson plans for my classes in seminary.

Through the rush of these pressures, although they were all directed toward the work of the Lord's kingdom, I had overextended myself and was finding it increasingly difficult to find time to communicate meaningfully with Him. As a consequence I was probably doing less than my best in each capacity, and my own spiritual well-being was suffering as a consequence.

Therefore, even in a Church experience we must be careful that we do not mistake purposeless activity for a state of spiritual well-being. The Master himself emphatically stressed the necessity of the development of the inner life as well as outward activity. Unless the inner self is being enriched and nourished by our activity, is it not possible that such outward efforts are sometimes in vain? The focus of the Master, it seems to me, was always on the inner man, on the heart and the soul, rather than on that which was experienced only at the exterior.

My second point, therefore, is that quietude is a vital prerequisite for communion with God. Unless inner peace is evident, the cares of the world—in a religious setting as well as a secular setting—can drown out the promptings of the still, small voice of the Spirit. If the Master needed frequently to escape the crowds that assembled around him, and if Joseph Smith needed the solitude of the grove away from his home, how much greater is our need to create those silent moments of escape, physically and emotionally?[5]

Each of us may wish to ask ourselves this very important question: "Are there too many programs, activities or meetings in my life

5. Arthur R. Bassett, "Before Praying," *Ensign,* Jan. 1976, 31.

such that they are interfering with my receiving communications from the Holy Ghost or the whisperings of the Spirit?" If so, then just like peeling back the layers of an onion, one needs to start peeling back the noisy layers of this busy world to expose and amplify the expressions of the still small voice and other promptings of the Spirit.

The elimination of these extraneous noises will be accomplished in different ways on different days. I find a level of quietude while driving my car. Some days while driving to work in the morning, I like to turn the cell phone and car radio off. I can then spend 25 minutes in personal thought or vocal prayer. I recall other times when I would drive from Lubbock to Sweetwater, Texas. I would often make the three-hour drive without listening to the car radio. This allowed me to use that time to think and pray vocally. I still do that when I drive alone for extended periods of time. I love to pray out loud, especially for members of my family—giving thanks for each one of them and praying for their particular wants and needs.

Others may have similar places of quietude, including in their car, at home, at church, an office, in the woods behind one's house, or in the temple.[6] While some places may be more conducive to a spirit of quietude than others, there are many places where an atmosphere of quietude may be experienced, resulting in an enhanced ability to hear the sacred expressions of the Spirit delivering personal revelation.

Secret Prayer

Another element to consider when preparing to communicate with Diety is deciding where one ought to be when offering a prayer. If there is a prayer in one's heart continually, perhaps it goes without saying that it is not possible to have a preferred location for the offering of any prayer. It also goes without saying that one cannot suggest only one location for all prayers. However, certain more formal or special prayers may require a special place. For example, Jesus, in Gethsemane, was "at the place." (Luke 22:40) Joseph Smith went "to the place where I had previously designed to go."

6. Alma 5:57.

(Joseph Smith—History 1:15) It is not suggested that a specific place be selected for the offering of special prayers; however, there is a type of place that can be suggested as appropriate for prayer. This type of place will be where one can literally be apart from the world—almost any quiet, secluded, secret place will do.[7]

Seclusion is an element worth serious consideration. If we look to the Savior as our example, we see that he prayed in seclusion in the desert, in the hills and in the mountains.[8] There were special occasions where he prayed while his disciples were present or within earshot, as he did at the Last Supper and in Gethsemane.[9] But there is no evidence that he ever prayed, however briefly, in the presence of any hecklers or nonbelievers. This suggests that we should be cautious about where we pray. With rare exceptions, it most likely is not appropriate to bow one's head in an overt manner in a public restaurant and ask for a blessing on the food. Some feel that such prayerful displays are just that—displays—no matter how well-intentioned the prayer might be. Despite one's feelings on this subject, the scriptures teach: "And again, I command thee that thou shalt pray vocally as well as in thy heart; yea, before the world as well as in secret, in public as well as in private." (D&C 19:28) It is good that we have the Savior's example to follow regarding this practice.

On one occasion I was out of town attending a business seminar along with twelve of our company's managers and executives. Late in the afternoon we received a report that one of our co-worker's, Ruth's, husband had passed away that day. A little later that evening, while our group was gathered in the waiting area of a noisy restaurant, there was a great deal of discussion about our friend and her latest loss. In contrast to the lively atmosphere of the Italian restaurant, the mood of our group was more subdued.

The large table around which we sat was located in the middle of one of the restaurant's busy serving areas. As we talked about Ruth and her third immediate-family death in the last six months, one of

---

7. 3 Nephi 13:5-6.
8. Mark 1:35; Luke 5:16; Luke 6:12.
9. Luke 22:19-20, 39-46.

our company's owners suggested that we have a prayer for Ruth, and asked me to offer the prayer. Notwithstanding my personal views about praying in public, I felt comfortable and honored to be asked to pray for our friend and her family, in spite of our public surroundings.

A more compelling reason for praying in secret is explained in Doctrine and Covenants 6:16: "Yea, I tell thee, that thou mayest know that there is none else save God that knowest thy thoughts and the intents of thy heart."[10] Thus, praying in secret may be interpreted to mean praying in silence. According to Elder Francis M. Gibbons,

> God has provided a channel of communication between him and his children on earth that Satan, our common enemy cannot invade. This is the channel of secret prayer. The significance of this to the Latter-day Saint is profound, for by this means we are able to communicate with our Heavenly Father in secrecy, confident that the adversary cannot intrude."[11]

As a means of getting away from the world and being secluded, many have literally gone to the mountains or some other high place to pray. It is difficult to understand this phenomenon, but from Old Testament times to the present, there has been a yearning in the hearts and minds of many to go to the mountains to pray. For some, this is a means of finding the necessary seclusion—that secret place. For others, it is a desire to get closer to, and feel the grandeur of God.[12] Is it even possible for anyone to view the panorama from a mountaintop, from a tall office building or from an airplane, and not know that there is a God, that he loves us and hears and answers our prayers?

---

10. See also 1 Kings 8:39; 2 Chronicles 6:30.

11. Francis M. Gibbons, "The Dual Aspects of Prayer," *Ensign,* Nov. 1991, 78.

12. "And they rose up early in the morning, and gat them up into the top of the mountain." (Numbers 14:40) "And I, Nephi, did go into the mount oft, and I did pray oft unto the Lord; wherefore the Lord showed unto me great things." (1 Nephi 18:3)

As a teenager, I once found seclusion in the living room of our home. I remember sitting in one of the living room chairs, closing my eyes and plugging my ears with my hands as I prayed. Even though there were others in the house, I felt secluded from everyone and everything else.

Another place where there is an abundance of quiet and seclusion may be the temple. Everyone who walks through the doors of the temple crosses a threshold to a place where the world is excluded. Within those sacred walls, there are many opportunities to pray silently while in sacred seclusion. As Ezra Taft Benson teaches,

> In the peace of these lovely temples, sometimes we find solutions to the serious problems of life. Under the influence of the Spirit, sometimes pure knowledge flows to us there. Temples are places of personal revelation. When I have been weighed down by a problem or a difficulty, I have gone to the house of the Lord with a prayer in my heart for answers. These answers have come in clear and unmistakable ways."[13]

Another benefit from praying in secret is the privilege of kneeling down before our Father in Heaven. A gesture, as simple as kneeling, inspires within us a feeling of humility before our Maker. It shows that we have within us the sincere feeling that compared to ourselves, God truly is great, that we are dependent upon him for everything, including life itself. Such a gesture and feeling on our part allows us to more easily offer up the desires of our heart to God.[14]

Pray Always

The commandment is simple and clear: "I say unto you that ye must pray always." (2 Nephi 32:9; See also 2 Nephi 9:52; 3 Nephi 20:1; Ephesians 6:18) Always means always, continually, and unceasingly. Does that mean every moment of every hour, twenty-four hours a day, every day?

---

13. Reed A. Benson, *The Teachings of Ezra Taft Benson,* Salt Lake City: Bookcraft, 1988, 251.

14. See Luke 22:41; Joseph Smith—History 1:15; 3 Nephi 17:13,15; 19:6-8, 16-17; Moroni 4:2.

It is the general practice of church members to have a family prayer at least once, if not twice a day—in the morning and in the evening. To those prayers can be added morning and evening personal prayers, the blessing on the food at mealtimes, and the prayers offered at various church meetings or other gatherings. All of these prayers are desirable and encouraged. Blessed is the person who participates in such prayers on a daily basis. Are they not enough? No, they are not enough. These prayers serve as the day-to-day backbone and framework upon which all other prayers rest.

This concept is taught well by the prophet Amulek in the Book of Mormon. He tells us to cry unto God morning, mid-day and evening.[15] And when we are not crying unto the Lord, Amulek tells us that we should continue to pray by letting our "hearts be full, drawn out in prayer unto him continually." (Alma 34:27) In spite of how clear the directive to "pray always" may be, many people do not realize that there are many specific blessings that come from praying continually. Here are some of the blessings delineated in the scriptures that come to us when we pray always:

- We will escape the evils of this life and be found worthy to stand before the Son of man. (Luke 21:36)
- The Father will consecrate our personal actions, that our performance may be for the welfare of our souls. (2 Nephi 32:9)
- God will hear our prayers. (2 Nephi 33:3)
- We will not be tempted beyond our capacity to bear it and will thus be led by the Holy Spirit, becoming humble, meek, submissive, patient, full of love and all long-suffering. (Alma 13:28, 34:39)
- We may know the mysteries of God and have things revealed to us that never have been revealed. It shall be given to us to bring thousands of souls to repentance. (Alma 26:22)
- We will wax strong and prosper in the land. (Alma 62:51)
- We will not be tempted and led away by the devil. We will conquer Satan and will escape the grasping hands of his

15. Alma 34:21.

servants. We will have power over the wicked one. (3 Nephi 18:15, 18, D&C 10:5, 31:12, 93:49)

- We will know what we should pray for. (3 Nephi 19:24) This is especially important when we are about to perform a priesthood ordinance. Is there a better reason to do this than that we might know what to say when performing such an ordinance? (Moroni 2:2, 3:2)
- The Savior will pour out his Spirit upon us—a blessing greater than if we were to receive the riches of this world. (D&C 19:38)
- We will have an understanding of the written revelations, the scriptures. (D&C 32:4)
- We will be able to abide the day of the Lord's coming, whether in life or in death. (D&C 61:39)
- We will have the necessary physical and spiritual strength to sustain us until the Savior comes and receives us to himself. (D&C 88:126)
- All things shall work together for our good. (D&C 90:24)

The Savior is the ultimate example of one who prayed continually. The words of Bruce R. McConkie describe the Savior's practice:

> As an obedient son whose sole desire was to do the will of the Father who sent him, our Lord prayed always and often during his mortal probation. By natural inheritance, because God was his Father, Jesus was endowed with greater powers of intellect and spiritual insight than anyone else has ever possessed. But in spite of his superlative natural powers and endowments—or, shall we not rather say, because of them (for truly the more spiritually perfected and intellectually gifted a person is, the more he recognizes his place in the infinite scheme of things and knows thereby his need for help and guidance from Him who truly is infinite)—and so by virtue of his superlative powers and endowments, Jesus above all men felt the need for constant communion with the Source of all power, all intelligence, and all goodness.[16]

---

16. Bruce R. McConkie, "Why the Lord Ordained Prayer," *Ensign,* Jan. 1976, 7.

Like the Savior, everybody can pray always. Prayers can be offered regularly, consistently, every day without fail. Everyone can also live with a prayerful spirit always in his or her heart, such that one's thoughts, words, and acts are always of a manner that will please God. Whether it is realized or not, some of our thoughts are prayers. There are many times when, notwithstanding the activity of the physical body, our spirit is kneeling in prayer. Consequently, we may not realize the many times throughout a day that we are actually praying.

Such informal prayers are often reflexive or reactionary pleas for help or expressions of thanks, offered as the occasion requires, indicating, spontaneously, that there truly is a prayer in our heart—that we are praying always. I often experience this type of spontaneous prayer when I see someone who is physically or mentally disabled. I reflexively express my gratitude for my own physical or mental wellbeing. If I am not thinking selfishly, I will offer a prayer for the disabled person whom I presume to be less fortunate than me. I have had similar experiences while driving, when I realize I just barely escaped getting into an auto accident. I instinctively offer a quick prayer of thanks, that I avoided the accident and was not hurt. Many others have had experiences similar to mine—remember the dreaded "pop" quiz in high school—the one for which we "forgot" to prepare? Such spontaneous prayers for divine intervention or assistance demonstrate that one's heart truly is in the right place.

Everyone can have a prayer in his or her heart while walking the dog, driving to work, waiting in a doctor's or dentist's office, standing in line at the theatre, or lying in bed trying to fall asleep. One of the best ways for a person's heart to be drawn out unto God continually is to spend time identifying those things for which one is grateful. While walking the dog, one is grateful for the ability to walk or the beauty of local surroundings. While driving to work one is thankful for his or her physical ability to judge distances. In the doctor's office, one can express gratitude for the progress of medical science. In line at the theater, one can appreciate his or her uniqueness as a child of God among the billions of his children. While struggling to fall asleep, one can be grateful that the mattress is soft and that there is safety and security inside a warm house.

In summary, Alma said it best, "Yea, and cry unto God for all thy support; yea, let all thy doings be unto the Lord, and whithersoever thou goest let it be in the Lord; yea, let all thy thoughts be directed unto the Lord; yea, let the affections of thy heart be placed upon the Lord forever. Counsel with the Lord in all thy doings, and he will direct thee for good; yea, when thou liest down at night lie down unto the Lord, that he may watch over you in your sleep; and when thou risest in the morning let thy heart be full of thanks unto God." (Alma 37:36-37)

Preparation is a Continual Process

Preparation for prayer is not passive; it is an active process. Those who are seeking to do God's will are constantly improving and refining their temperament and character in an effort to become more Christ-like. Such individuals will find themselves seeking the Lord early, praying in places or circumstances of quietude, praying in secret and praying always.

Although most people will not instantaneously acquire all the character traits of a true seeker of God's will, everyone can immediately begin making little adjustments that will draw him closer to the Christ-like character he seeks. Since no one is perfect, it is understood that we do not need to be perfect or always perfectly prepared to receive answers to our prayers. However, the more prepared we are, the better the two-way communication between man and Heavenly Father will be.[17] It is abundantly clear that there is an answer to *every* prayer; consequently, there must even be an answer to every prayer offered by he or she who is imperfectly prepared.

The struggle many experience in receiving answers to their prayers may have less to do with their personal preparation than it does with their willingness to put aside their personal wants and desires and their committing to follow the Lord's will for them. Of course, the better an individual prepares for prayer, the greater will be the individual's desire to yield to God's will.

---

17. "God reveals himself to [people] who are prepared for such manifestations." *Conference Report,* Salt Lake City: The Church of Jesus Christ of Latter-day Saints, Apr. 1964, 97.

What should people do who try to prepare for prayer the best way they know how, yet cannot find the desire to pray? Whenever they do not feel like praying, then they need to follow President Ezra Taft Benson's advice to "pray until we do feel like praying. We should be humble. We should pray for forgiveness and mercy. We must forgive anyone against whom we have bad feelings."[18]

Proper preparation for prayer will stimulate every individual to strive to live a Christ-like life. Such preparation will enable everyone to know what to pray for, how to pray and how to be prepared for the answer when it is provided—in no matter which of the many forms the answer may come. Whatever preparations an individual can make will take that person closer, in a unique way, to receiving discernable answers to prayers.

18. Ezra Taft Benson, "Pray Always," *Ensign,* Feb, 1990, 4.

4
The Prayer

Learning How to Pray

My father, Warren R. Young, was born and reared in Salt Lake City, Utah, as a member of The Church of Jesus Christ of Latter-day Saints. My mother, Alice Bell, was born and reared in Minneapolis, Minnesota, as a member of the Methodist church. My parents met during the early years of World War II, while each served as officers in the United States Marine Corps. My church membership records show that soon after my birth, my grandfather, Harold E. Young, gave me a name and a blessing.

Notwithstanding my LDS Church heritage, my early childhood years were not spent as a member of the church. In fact, my first experiences with church and religious teachings came from my mother and her Protestant associations. As a child, I recall attending the Minneapolis Hennepin Avenue Methodist Church. Even though we may not have been regular attendees of that or any other church, my mother taught me about prayer and how to pray.

My mother believed in God and believed in prayer. She taught my sisters and me to pray each night before we went to sleep. I would put on my blue "feet pajamas," crawl into my bed, and wait while my mom tucked the covers in tightly around me. Then, I would say this prayer out loud:

> Now I lay me down to sleep.
> I pray the Lord my soul to keep.
> If I should die before I wake,
> I pray the Lord my soul to take.
> Amen.

My mother also taught us to be grateful for our blessings—especially our food. At every meal, we would ask for a blessing on the food, by saying this prayer:

> God is great, God is good,
> And we thank him for this food.
> By his hand we must be fed.
> Give us, Lord, our daily bread.
> Amen.

When I was 12 years old, my mother, my sisters, and I were baptized members of The Church of Jesus Christ of Latter-day Saints. As was the nature of our family, we became diligent and faithful church attendees. With the exception of a six-month period when I was in the seventh grade, I cannot recall a time that our family stayed home on a Sunday rather than attending church. As a consequence of our church activity, our routine blessings on the food began to be less rote and to have more spiritual substance. Before we knew it, we had adopted the general LDS format for the blessings on our food. We had progressed to a new level of routine, mechanical mealtime prayers, which when offered went something like this:

> Dear Heavenly Father, we thank thee for this food and ask thee to bless it, to nourish and strengthen our bodies and do us the good we need. In the name of Jesus Christ, Amen.

If we really wanted to give a display of our spiritual maturity, we would interject a phrase such as, "and please bless the hands that prepared it." I am sure that most of us have heard a variation of this prayer more than once. Over time and with increased age, my routine mealtime prayers have become more meaningful expressions of gratitude, with less repetition and more heartfelt thanks for the bounties of the earth.

Most of my other prayers followed a similar growth pattern, a pattern where my prayers became less mechanical and more heartfelt. When I think of the many routine prayers that I offered, I am glad that I prayed, but I feel somewhat embarrassed that it took me so many years to let my natural sincerity take over from my vain repetitions. When you think of your own mechanical, vain repetitions, perhaps you can imagine one of your night-time prayers going something like the prayer that follows. I do not share this sample prayer with you out of any intent to be disrespectful. Notwithstanding the irreverence displayed at times in this prayer, it is a prayer from which lessons may be learned:

A Nighttime Prayer—Interrupted

My Dear Father in Heaven . . .

• Yes?

Don't interrupt me. I'm praying.

• But you called me.

Called You? I didn't call you. I'm praying . . . My Dear Father in Heaven . . .

• There, you did it again.

Did what?

• Called me. You said, "My Dear Father in Heaven." Here I am. What's on your mind?

But I didn't mean anything by it. I was just, You know, saying my prayers for the night. I always say my prayers. It makes me feel good, kind of like getting my duty done.

• Oh. All Right. Go on.

I'm thankful for my many blessings . . .

• Hold it. How thankful?

What?

• How thankful are you for your "many blessings?"

I'm . . . well . . . I don't know. How should I know? It's just part of the prayer. Everyone always said that I should express my thanks.

• Oh well. You're welcome. Go ahead . . .

Go ahead?

• With the prayer.

Oh yeah. Let's see . . . bless the poor and the sick and the needy and the afflicted . . .

• Do you really mean that?

Well, sure I mean it.

• What are you doing about it?

Doing? Who, me? Nothing, I guess. I just think that it would be kind of nice if You got control of things down here like You have up there, so people don't have to suffer so.

• Have I got control of you?

Well I go to church, I pay my tithing, I don't . . .

• That isn't what I asked you. What about your temper? You have a problem there, and your friends and family suffer. And then there's the way you spend your money . . . all on yourself. And how about the kinds of books you read?

Stop picking on me. I'm just as good as some of the rest of those I see every Sunday at church.

• Excuse Me. I thought you were praying for me to bless the needy. If that is going to happen, I'll have to have help from the ones who are praying for it . . . like you.

All right. I guess that I have a few hang-ups, now that you mention it. I could probably mention some others.

• So could I.

Look, Father. I need to finish up here. This is taking a lot longer than usual. Bless the missionaries to be led to the doors of the honest in heart.

• You mean people like Ralph?

Ralph?

• Yes, the guy around the corner.

"That" Ralph? But he smokes and drinks and never goes to church.

• Have you looked in his heart lately?

Of course not. How can . . .

• I have. I looked. And it's one of those honest hearts you were just praying about.

O.K. then, get the missionaries over there. Do you think I like having a non-member for a neighbor?

• Aren't you supposed to be a missionary? I thought I made that pretty clear.

Hey, wait a minute. What is this? Criticize "me" day? Here I am, doing my duty, keeping your commandments to pray. And all of a sudden you break in and start reminding me of all my problems.

• Well, you called me. And here I am. Keep on praying. I'm interested in this next part. You haven't changed the order around have you? Go on . . .

I don't want to.

• Why not?

I know what you'll say.

• Try Me and see.

Please forgive me of all my sins . . . and help me to forgive others.

• What about Bill?

See. I knew it. I knew you'd bring him up. Listen Lord, he told lies about me, and I got fired. All my co-workers think I'm a first-class creep, and I didn't do anything. I'm going to get even with him!

• But your prayers. What about your prayers?

I didn't mean it.

• Well, at least you're honest. I guess you enjoy carrying that load of bitterness around, don't you?

No, I don't. But I'll feel better as soon as I get even.

• Do you want to know a secret?

What secret?

• You won't feel better. You'll feel worse. Listen to me. You forgive Bill and I'll forgive you.

But Lord, I can't forgive Bill.

• Then I cannot forgive you.

No matter what?

• No matter what. But you're not through with your prayer yet. Go on.

Oh all right . . . please help me to control my feelings and not yield to temptations.

• Good. Good. I'll do just that. But you stop putting yourself in all those places where you can be tempted.

What do you mean by that?

• Quit hanging around the magazine racks and spending so much time in front of the tube. Some of that stuff is going to get to you sooner or later. You'll find yourself involved in some terrible things before long . . . and don't use me for an escape hatch either.

An escape hatch? I don't understand.

• Sure you do. You've done it lots of times—you find yourself in a crisis situation, then you come running to me. "Lord, help me out of this mess and I promise I'll never do it again." It's amazing how the quality and intensity of your prayers improve when you are in trouble. Do you remember some of those bargains you tried to make with me?

Well I don't think . . . Oh . . . yeah . . . like the time Mom's visiting teacher saw me coming out of that movie about . . . Oh brother . . .

• Do you remember your prayer? I do. "Oh God. Don't let her tell my mother where I've been. I promise I'll go to nothing but "G" rated movies from now on. She didn't tell your mother, but you didn't keep your promise. Did you?

No Lord, I didn't. I'm sorry.

• So am I. Go ahead and finish your prayer.

Wait a minute. I want to ask you a question. Do you always listen to my prayers?

• Every word. Every time.

Then how come you never talked back to me before?

• How many chances have you given me? There's not enough time between your "Amens" and your head hitting the pillow for me to draw a breath. How am I supposed to give an answer?

You could, if you really wanted to.

• No. I could if *you* really wanted me to. Child, I always want to.

Father, I am sorry. Will you forgive me?

• I already have. And thanks for letting me interrupt. I get lonely to talk to you sometimes. Goodnight. I love you.

Good night, and I love you too.

Amen.[1]

Like the prayer-giver in the above fictitious example, many of my prayers, personal and public, have also evolved, some reaching the level of genuine two-way communication with my Father in Heaven. I see this development in prayer as a mini law of

1. Author unknown. Circulated via email on the Internet.

prayerful progression. Generally, prayers progress from the mechanical (telestial), to the one-way, heartfelt expression (terrestrial), to genuine, two-way communication with our Heavenly Father (celestial).[2]

So that all prayers can become celestial in nature—genuine, two-way communications with God, as one person communicates with another—it is important to examine the key elements of a properly offered prayer. These key elements include the following:

- We pray out of faith.
- We pray by the power of the Holy Ghost.
- We pray with real intent.
- We pray to God the Father.
- We express our gratitude.
- We pray for that which is right, good and expedient.
- We pray that our Father's will be done.
- We pray in the name of Jesus Christ.
- We say, "Amen."

We Pray Out of Faith

Every time someone prays, it demonstrates by that act that he or she loves God and that he or she has faith that He exists and is listening to his or her prayer. Since the depth of one's faith can vary, one is more likely to receive a discernable answer to a prayer if the prayer is offered because the person possesses a deep rather than a doubting faith. As the scriptures teach, one is powerless without faith: "Remember that without faith you can do nothing; therefore ask in faith." (D&C 8:10) However, according to the Savior, faith is the ingredient that gives us the power to do the will of the Lord.

---

2. See Stephen R. and Sandra Covey, "Teaching Our Children to Pray," *Ensign,* Jan. 1976, 59. Also, Joseph Smith once said, "it is the first principle of the gospel to know for a certainty the character of God, and to know that we may converse with Him as one man converses with another." (*History of the Church,* 6:305)

"And Christ hath said: If ye will have faith in me ye shall have power to do whatsoever thing is expedient in me." (Moroni 7:33)

When there is sufficient faith to activate that enabling power and ask the Father in the name of the Son for that which is good, then whatsoever one shall ask shall be done. This is confirmed by the scripture that teaches, "Whatsoever thing ye shall ask the Father in my name, which is good, in faith believing that ye shall receive, behold, it shall be done unto you." (Moroni 7:26) In addition to receiving the requested answer to a prayer, when a person has faith and asks for good things, that person is blessed with the Holy Ghost.

We Pray by the Power of the Holy Ghost

One often-overlooked guideline for effective prayer is prayer by the power of the Holy Ghost. This is the highest achievement in prayer. The promise from the scriptures is: "The Spirit shall be given unto you by the prayer of faith," (D&C 42:14) "and if ye are purified and cleansed from all sin, ye shall ask whatsoever you will in the name of Jesus and it shall be done." (D&C 50:29)

The Savior has instructed that everyone is to ask the Father in Jesus' name, "in faith believing that you shall receive, and you shall have the Holy Ghost, which manifesteth all things which are expedient unto the children of men." (D&C 18:18) Without the aid of the Holy Ghost no one can know the will of God. When an individual prays by the power of the Holy Ghost, that person knows he or she is in harmony with the will of the Father. That individual should not only pray to obtain the guidance of the Holy Ghost in his life, that person should pray for the guidance and influence of the Holy Ghost in the offering of every prayer.

Those that pray by the power of the Holy Ghost are praying as God would have them pray.[3] Communicating with God the Father under such a divine influence, one's personal prayer in essence becomes God's prayer, because the person will be praying for only those things about which God desires that we pray. Naturally, one may want to ask, "Do I have to pray God's way and say what he

3. D&C 46:30.

wants me to say, in order for my prayer to be answered? If I pray only as guided by the Holy Ghost, then is it really my prayer? When do I get to offer my own prayer, to ask for things that I want?"

Perhaps these questions are answered with this question: whose will do you want to be done—yours or Heavenly Father's? If people want the will of the Father to be done, and if they want the answer to their prayers to be guided by the Holy Spirit, then the Holy Spirit must likewise guide the prayer that seeks such an answer. In the offering of prayers, The Savior promises that the Holy Ghost will be sent by the Father to teach all things, and bring all things to one's remembrance.[4] Consistent with this promise, the Savior teaches that, "If ye abide in me, and my words abide in you, ye shall ask what ye will, and it shall be done unto you." (John 15:7) Through this process, everyone can learn the value of trusting in and relying upon Heavenly Father's plan for him or her, rather than pressing him to answer their prayers in accordance with their personal agendas and narrow perspectives. By yielding to the influence of the Holy Ghost in the offering of a prayer, one will realize that he or she will know the will of God before he or she asks for it. Such truth will be made known by the power of the Holy Ghost, and by the power of the Holy Ghost one may know the truth of all things.[5] Having all things made known in such a manner enables a person to be the recipient of portions of the infinite knowledge of God.

We Pray With Real Intent

One day, one of my sons, a senior in high school, asked, "Dad, how do you know you are praying with real intent?" In reply, I told him that one prays with real intent when one is sincerely honest in one's heart, feelings and expressions. I think my son knew the answer to his question before he asked it. I say that because I believe that in our respective heart of hearts, we all know whether we are praying with real intent. Such personal awareness has always been with each of us. Mark Twain expresses this point simply and clearly through

4. John 14:26.
5. Moroni 10:4-5.

Huckleberry Finn, one of the characters in his book, *The Adventures of Huckleberry Finn:*

> It made me shiver. And I about made up my mind to pray and see if I couldn't try to quit bein' the kind of a boy I was and be better. So I kneeled down, But the words wouldn't come. Why wouldn't they? It weren't no use to try and hide it from Him. . . . I knowed very well why they wouldn't come. It was because my heart warn't right; it was because I warn't square; it was because I was playin' double. I was lettin' on to give up sin, but way inside of me I was holdin' on to the biggest one of all. I was tryin' to make my mouth say I would do the right thing and the clean thing . . . but deep down in me I knowed it was a lie, and He knowed it. You can't pray a lie. I found that out.[6]

While Huck Finn states it clearly, there is more to this concept than not praying a lie. We need to pray honestly, being willing to follow the will of the Father with our whole heart, without hypocrisy or deception in our thoughts or actions.[7]

There are plusses and minuses to praying with real intent. On the plus side, the fervent, passionate, honest prayer will be of great help to the person offering such a prayer.[8] A prayer offered sincerely, with real intent, with faith in Christ, results in God revealing his truth by the power of the Holy Ghost, by which power one may know the truth of all things.[9] As seekers of truth and light, is this not one of the greatest of all blessings with which one could be blessed? An additional blessing that is granted to those who pray with real intent is the Lord's promise that he will be merciful to us.[10]

While there is a marvelous upside to praying with real intent, the prophet Moroni provides a warning to those who pray without real intent. To such people he warns, "And likewise also is it counted evil

---

6. Mark Twain, "The Adventures of Huckleberry Finn," *The Portable Mark Twain,* New York: The Viking Press, 1968, 449. See also Alma 18:32.
7. See 2 Nephi 31:13.
8. James 5:16.
9. Moroni 10:4-5.
10. Helaman 3:27.

unto a man, if he shall pray and not with real intent of heart; yea, and it profiteth him nothing, for God receiveth none such." (Moroni 7:9) When someone prays without real intent, it is reasonable to conclude that such a prayer falls into the category of a vain repetition. This should not be allowed to happen. Therefore, one must always strive diligently to follow Moroni's counsel and "pray unto the Father with all the energy of heart." (Moroni 7:48)

The Savior is the best example of one who applies the principle of praying with real intent. While pouring out his soul to his Father in the Garden of Gethsemane, he suffered in a manner that mankind may never know or fully understand. Notwithstanding his incomprehensible agony, he prayed with great fervor. In the middle of these events, an angel appeared to him and strengthened him. Being in agony, the scriptures record that Jesus "prayed more earnestly." (Luke 22:42-44) A couple of important lessons may be learned from this account. First, one learns that the Savior, whose every prayer was always perfectly worded and perfectly accentuated, offered his prayers earnestly. Second, this account teaches that all prayers, the Savior's included, are not alike. At times, a greater need requires an even greater faith-filled and earnest petition before the throne of that divine being who desires to answer all such petitions.

Real intent does not come from the words one chooses to use in a prayer. Such earnestness comes from the candid, honest feelings—the yearnings of the soul—that are felt as one pours out the simple sentiments of the heart to God. Our words may be simple and unrefined; however, our Heavenly Father will receive the real intent of our hearts as communications of divine, spiritual eloquence.

We Pray to God the Father

To whom should we pray? The answer to that question was first given to Adam and Eve, who were instructed to "Call upon God in the name of the Son forevermore." (Moses 5:8) The answer first given to Adam and Eve was ratified by the Savior's own practice, as exemplified in The Lord's Prayer—we should always pray to God, our Father who is in heaven. The instruction is simple and clear: we must *always* pray unto the Father in the name of the Son.[11] During

11. 3 Nephi 18:19, emphasis added. See also Matt 6:6; 2 Nephi 32:9; 3 Ne 13:6, 18:23, 30, 19:6-8, 19-21, 20:31; Moroni 4:2, 7:48.

the Savior's visit to the Nephites in the Americas, he gave them specific instructions regarding the manner of prayer, and he showed them by his own example how to pray to the Father in the name of the Son.

Notwithstanding his instructions and his personal example, some of the Nephites proceeded to pray directly to Jesus—something many people may have heard once or twice in various settings. The Savior did not express any displeasure with the Nephites because they had erroneously prayed to him rather than the Father. Shortly after Jesus heard the people pray to him rather than to his Father, Jesus prayed to his Father on their behalf. Acting in his role as their advocate before the Father, Jesus explained why the Nephites prayed to him (Jesus) rather than to their Heavenly Father. Jesus simply stated, "They pray unto me because I am with them." (3 Nephi 19:22)

By praying directly to Jesus rather than to his Father, the Nephites did not commit an offence or oversight of grave consequence. It may very well be that their prayer under such circumstances represents an instance where it is fully acceptable to pray to the Son—when he is physically present, representing himself as well as the Father. Perhaps all would be so overcome by being in the Savior's physical presence that they too, would consider their prayer to the Savior to be synonymous with a prayer directly to the Father.

An impressive point about this experience is that the Savior did not let such an event pass without comment. It may be that one of Jesus' special assignments during his visit to the Americas was to teach the people how to pray. Therefore, it was important to Jesus that he point out to his Father that he was aware that the Nephite people were praying to someone other than the Father. By mentioning this concern to the Father in his prayer, Jesus was honoring the principle that he taught in his plan that he proposed in the pre-earthly existence—that all glory goes to the Father. As the Savior proposed, lived and continues to teach today, he does not take upon himself any honor that is due the Father.

I have several friends and relatives who have lost loved ones. These friends and relatives do not pray to their loved ones, but I am aware that they direct some of their conversations to them. Often such conversations focus on how much they love and miss the departed and wish that the loved one were still alive to help the surviving person cope with certain struggles of life. I do not believe we should be critical of those engaging in such conversations. Similarly, we must keep in mind that we are not prohibited from conversing with the Savior, as our brother, expressing our love to him and expressing a desire for his help with our daily struggles. Whatever the proper perspective is on this point, the scriptures and church leaders have always taught that all prayers should be offered to the Father, in the name of the Son.

I like the way one scholar summarizes this key principle:

> We are commanded to pray to the Father in the name of the Son. It is true that when we pray to the Father, the answer comes from the Son, because "there is … one mediator between God and men, the man Christ Jesus." (1Tim. 2:5) Joseph Smith, for instance, asked the Father, in the name of the Son, for answers to questions, and the answering voice was not that of the Father but of the Son, because Christ is our advocate, our intercessor, the God (under the Father) who rules and regulates this earth. And it is true that sometimes in his answers, Christ assumes the prerogative of speaking by divine investiture of authority as though he were the Father; that is, he speaks in the first person and uses the name of the Father because the Father has placed his own name on the Son. For a full explanation of this see the official pronouncement, "The Father and The Son: A Doctrinal Exposition by The First Presidency and The Twelve," beginning on page 465 of the book *Articles of Faith* by Elder James E. Talmage. But what we must have perfectly clear is that we always pray to the Father, not the Son, and we always pray in the name of the Son.[12]

In all communications with Heavenly Father, one should remember to use the proper reverential pronouns *thee, thou, thy* and *thine.* The casual personal pronouns *you* and *your* should be avoided. For some people, it may take some getting used to; however, the uses of

12. Bruce R. McConkie, "Why the Lord Ordained Prayer," *Ensign,* Jan. 1976, 7.

thee, thou, thy and *thine* will soon become natural and allow the giver of the prayer to converse in a trusting and sincere manner as one would with friends or family.

Now, an important word of caution: It is very easy to overuse the words, God, Father, Heavenly Father, Lord, etc., in our prayers. It is sufficient to use a reference to Heavenly Father once as we begin our prayer and use the name of Jesus Christ only once as we close the prayer. The names of Deity should not be casually or vainly repeated throughout the prayer.

We Express Our Gratitude

As I write this section of the book, I do so on a most appropriate day—Thanksgiving. Like so many on this day, I am filled with gratitude for my life and the blessings of life. I am grateful that I am thankful enough to give thanks. Many are grateful; however, many are not grateful enough to express—openly or silently—that gratitude to our Heavenly Father, who provides all the blessings we experience. The need to express our gratitude is spelled out in the scriptures: "In every thing give thanks: for this is the will of God in Christ Jesus concerning you." (1 Thessalonians 5:18) In another verse of scripture, the advice is stern: "And in nothing doth man offend God, or against none is his wrath kindled, save those who confess not his hand in all things, and obey not his commandments." (D&C 59:21) While such language seems almost harsh, it contains a blessing worth noting. By keeping his commandments and acknowledging his hand in all things, including our successes, good deeds and challenges, we are protected against his wrath. That last scripture is weighty. By doing our best to keep God's commandments, and by continually expressing our gratitude, we can walk confidently through the day, knowing that our Father in Heaven is pleased with us.

Obviously, gratitude is one of the key elements of an effective prayer. As a person learns the basic format for offering a prayer, the person also learns to address the prayer to his or her Heavenly Father, expressing thanks for one's many blessings. One also learns to ask for those things that one may need, and then concludes the prayer in the name of Jesus Christ. When it comes to the purest substance in a prayer, perhaps all that a person really needs to do is call upon God, express his or her sincere thanks, and conclude in the name of Jesus Christ. One could often say: "I thank thee," "I am grateful," or, "I acknowledge before thee." If someone feels compelled to ask God for one thing, that one thing might be to know for what else he or she ought to express heartfelt gratitude. Summarizing the significance of gratitude in any communications with Heavenly Father, Meister Eckhart, a German theologian, may have said it best: "If the only prayer you ever say in your entire life is, 'Thank you,' it will be enough."[13]

When I was a full-time missionary, I somehow learned to recognize the importance of gratitude, especially as it relates to fasting and prayer. Like my fellow Elders and Sisters, I tried my best to find and teach effectively, to the end that we could baptize someone who wanted to be baptized. It was a constant struggle. My companions and I prayed continually to succeed in this effort. We prayed and fasted, and then we prayed and fasted some more. At some point, my asking and demanding finally gave way to gratitude. I suggested that my companion and I have a special fast for the sole purpose of expressing our thanks and gratitude to God for his many blessings. As a result of what I learned years ago, I still sometimes have a special fast for the sole purpose of thanking my Heavenly Father for answering my prayers and for his love, his many blessings and his generous mercy. I have fasted out of gratitude for the successful sale of a house, for the finding of a job, and for God's granting me one more day of life.[14]

There is always something for which a person can be grateful—even during times when that person may be experiencing such physical or emotional pain that it seems impossible. Many mornings, following a night of restless sleep, I have knelt down by the side of my bed and found that I can be grateful for the two hours of sleep I managed to get. After other similar experiences, I have been able to express my thanks for the little rest that I received, even though I may not have slept at all.

13. *Quotationary,* CD, NovaSoft 1999.
14. See Alma 19:14; Ether 6:9, 12.

Recognizing the importance of being grateful as well as the importance of expressing such gratitude in prayer, perhaps everyone should make the same pledge that Ammon made in the Book of Mormon: "I will give thanks unto my God forever." (Alma 26:37)

We Pray For That Which Is Right, Good and Expedient

There are so many elements that make up an effective prayer that it is difficult to give any one element singular importance. Yet, the element of "what" to pray for is unique and often overlooked. Many people pray with specific desires or requests in mind because they all have their specific problems or needs that they want addressed. In reality, they are only being self-centered in their prayers. Most people have a preconceived notion regarding the direction they presume their lives should take. As a consequence, they decide which of their selfish problems, hurdles or desires they should pray about, and how those problems, hurdles and desires should be handled or resolved. In the prayer process, these people seem to declare, "My way is the right way."

Since so many presume to know how their set of problems should be resolved, they conclude that they know the questions to ask God and the requests they should make of him in their prayers, believing they know the answers the Lord should give them. Such an attitude begs the asking of the following questions: "Are we, through our shortsightedness, trying to solicit from the Lord answers to meaningless questions? Are we trying to persuade him to deal with issues that are not in our best interest in an eternal sense? Is this the reason why the Lord seemingly has so little to say to us? Is this why we often find such little satisfaction from our prayers?"[15] Knowing, however, that the answers we get are determined in part by what we pray for, perhaps the dissatisfaction we experience with the answers we receive is a result of praying for the wrong thing. As summed up by the apostle Paul, "We know not what we should pray for as we ought." (Romans 8:26)

15. Arthur R. Bassett, "Before Praying," *Ensign,* Jan. 1976, 31.

The key to the "what" in the prayer process is to pray for the right thing. Of course this concept is taught in the scriptures: "And whatsoever ye shall ask the Father in my name, *which is right,* believing that ye shall receive, behold it shall be given unto you."[16] This point is corroborated in Moroni 7:26, "Whatsoever thing ye shall ask the Father in my name, *which is good,* in faith believing that ye shall receive, behold it shall be done unto you." This principle is reiterated to the prophet Joseph Smith, while at the same time, issuing a stern warning about the consequence for praying for the wrong thing: "Whatsoever ye ask the Father in my name it shall be given unto you, *that is expedient unto you.* And if ye ask anything that is not expedient for you, it shall turn unto your condemnation." (D&C 88:64-65)

If someone selfishly prays for anything that he or she may want, that person may forego an answer to his or her prayer. James, in the New Testament, sums it up this way, "Ye ask, and receive not, because ye ask amiss. . . ." (James 4:3) Knowing that one does not want to ask amiss, how does someone know what is right or expedient to pray for? It is simple. One prays to find out. That may cause someone to ask, "You mean, I have to pray to know what I should pray about?" Exactly. "Ask the Father in my name, in faith believing that you shall receive, and you shall have the Holy Ghost, *which manifesteth all things which are expedient* unto the children of men."[17] The prophet Nephi understood the importance of this principle when he said, "Yea, I know that God will give liberally to him that asketh. Yea, my God will give me, *if I ask not amiss.*"[18]

Here is a personal story to illustrate this point. Our daughter, together with her husband and young son, were driving from Arizona to Denver for a short vacation. We were so very anxious for them to visit us that we could hardly stand it. I remember praying for them to be blessed with two things. One, that they would arrive safely, and two, that their trip would be uneventful—free from mechanical breakdowns. Unfortunately, they had a severe mechanical problem

16. 3 Nephi 18:20; See also Moroni 7:26.
17. D&C 18:18; See also Romans 8:26-27.
18. 2 Nephi 4:35; See also James 4:3.

with their car that turned into a terrible experience for everyone involved. Thankfully, they finally made it to Denver safely. Since that memorable trip, I have wondered if perhaps I was praying for the wrong things, namely, incompatible results. Maybe, to ensure their safe arrival, the mechanical breakdown was required. I honestly do not know if this is so; nevertheless, of the two blessings I prayed for, I am most grateful that everyone arrived safe and sound.

In praying for that which is good and right, two things happen: (1) The person avoids praying for the wrong thing; (2) The prayer giver aligns himself with the will of God. In the Book of Mormon, this was confirmed to Nephi, the son of Helaman: "And now, because thou hast done this with such unwearyingness, behold, I will bless thee forever; and I will make thee mighty in word and in deed, in faith and in works; yea, even that all things shall be done unto thee according to thy word, for thou shalt not ask that which is contrary to my will." (Helaman 10:5) When one prays for the right thing, one is asking in accordance with the will of God.[19] As a consequence, "it is done even as he asketh." (D&C 46:30) If someone adopts the characteristics of a true seeker, that person will find this to be a true principle in the prayerful part of his or her daily life. "If ye are purified and cleansed from all sin, ye shall ask whatsoever you will in the name of Jesus and it shall be done. But know this, it shall be given you what you shall ask." (D&C 50:29-30)

We know that the blessing we receive by praying for that which is right and expedient is the granting of our prayer. Here is a short list of some of the right things for or about which we can pray:

- That we enter not into temptation. (Luke 22:46)
- Our children. (3 Nephi 17:21)
- Those that despitefully use us and persecute us. (3 Nephi 12:44; Matt 5:44)
- The strength to overcome our problems and afflictions. (Alma 31:31, 33)
- Success. (Alma 31:32)

19. 3 Nephi 13:8.

- Mercy, our households, against the power of our enemies, against the devil, the crops and flocks of our fields, our own welfare and the welfare of those around us. (Alma 34:17-27)
- That God will support us in our doings and direct us for good and watch over us in our sleep. (Alma 37:36-37)
- Our daily bread. (Matt. 6:11)
- Wisdom. (James 1:5)
- All things. (D&C 46:7); But note, "I pray not for the world, but for them which thou hast given me." (John 17:9)
- That our performance will be for the welfare of our own soul. (2 Nephi 32:9)
- That our wives and children may be blessed. (3 Nephi 18:21)
- For one another that we may be healed. (James 5:16)
- For those who attend our church meetings, members and non-members alike. (3 Nephi 18:22-23, 30)

Many, many years ago, Plato, the Greek philosopher, understood the need to pray for the right things and avoid praying for the wrong things. In his wisdom, he was cautious in what he prayed for. Prayed he: "Lord of Lords, grant us the good whether we pray for it or not, but evil keep from us, even though we pray for it."[20] The matters or concerns about which one prays should not be treated lightly. Modern scriptures tell us that we should "Trifle not with these things; do not ask for that which you ought not." (D&C 8:10) As we strive to pray for that which is right, let us ponder our concerns and circumstances, serve others, unwearyingly declare the word of God, fear not, put God's will ahead of our own life, keep the commandments, and let us not ask for that which is contrary to God's will.[21]

We Pray that the Father's Will Be Done

"Father, thy will be done." (Moses 4:2) These words were first uttered before anyone set foot on this earth. It should not surprise anyone that Jesus was the one who first voiced these words. The Savior next spoke these words when he gave what is known as the

---

20. *Quotationary,* CD, NovaSoft 1999.
21. Helaman 10:2-6; 3 Ne 19:24; D&C 46:30.

Lord's Prayer.[22] On yet another occasion, but this time in a moment of great agony in the garden of Gethsemane, the Savior again uttered his request that the will of the Father be done, notwithstanding his personal desires to have that bitter cup pass from him.[23] Is it clear what the Savior is trying to teach here? Jesus Christ—the First Born, the Beloved Son, he who was perfect in all things, he who could overcome all things—has from the beginning unfailingly yielded his will to that of his Father—our Father.

As an individual considers yielding his or her personal desires to the will of the Father, that person will see two challenges: First, that he must be willing to do the will of the Father. This is a challenge because the natural man is an enemy of God. Man's natural tendency is to seek his selfish desires and personal agenda. It takes discipline and a commitment to matters of the Spirit to conquer those natural tendencies so that the divine inclinations to serve God become one's predominant tendencies. The following quotation illustrates in a humorous way how man's natural tendencies impose on God's will for us: "Dear Lord, the gods have been good to me. As an offering, I present these milk and cookies. If you wish me to eat them instead, please give me no sign whatsoever . . . thy will be done—munch, munch, munch."[24]

The second challenge is that one must act—one must, by his or her own actions, do the will of the Father. The reason this is a challenge is because like the natural man, the spirit is willing but, often, the flesh is weak. Acting on new, divine inclinations requires faith, courage, willpower, and the capacity to withstand the slings and arrows of other natural men. This is not easy to do. Acting in a manner that is contrary to the world's views and popular convention is difficult. This is especially so when someone risks being labeled as strange, weird, fanatical, ultra-conservative, prudish, narrow-minded or some other humiliating name. It can be a most unsettling experience to do the will of God, knowing that such action may lead to feeling embarrassed or totally mortified.

---

22. Matthew 6:10; 3 Nephi 13:10.
23. Matthew. 26:39, 42.
24. *Quotationary,* CD, NovaSoft 1999.

While considering the faith and courage it takes to yield to the will of the Father, there is an appropriate verse from a poem by an unknown author:

> Each day I pray, God give me strength anew
> To do the tasks I do not wish to do;
> To yield obedience never asking why,
> To love and own the truth and scorn the lie.

Reflecting on the price that may have to be paid to do the will of the Father, strength may come by considering the agony of the Son of God in the Garden of Gethsemane. The Gethsemane principle can also be applied in our prayers. No matter how sincere a person may be in expressing the day's particular needs and desires, that person can always utter the following words: "Nevertheless, not as I will, but as thou wilt." The use of such an expression in prayer will directly affect the "who, what, why, when, where and how" that make up the contents of sincere prayers as well as the answers to those prayers.

We Pray in the Name of Jesus Christ

Since the time of Adam, the counsel has been given to offer all prayers in the name of the Son.[25] This counsel has been consistent throughout the scriptures. It is most clearly stated in 3 Nephi 18:19: "Therefore ye must always pray unto the Father in my name."[26]

We are commanded to pray in the name of Jesus Christ because he is our Mediator and Advocate with the Father. When we pray, our Lord may, in his role as Mediator, intercede on our behalf. He may help plead our case to the Father, strengthening our position as a seeker of truth and light. He may fulfill the required elements of an effectual prayer, by assuring that the prayer reaching the Father is full of faith, real intent and gratitude. It is as if a sincere and humble prayer is filtered through the Son, allowing him to make whole the

---

25. Moses 5:8.

26. See also John 14:13-14, 16, 16:23-26; 3 Nephi 17:3; 18: 20-21, 23, 30; 19:6-8, 19-21; 20:31; 32:9; Mormon 9:29; Moroni 4:2, 7:26; D&C 14:8, 18; 88:64.

infirmities of our prayer, interjecting for our benefit, "What Brother Young really means is. . . ."

By offering each prayer in the name of Jesus Christ, we are also reminded of his role as our Savior. He, as our Redeemer, through the Atonement and only through the Atonement, allows or causes our earthly, imperfect prayerful utterances to access the Father.

An important point to consider is that proper prayer includes all three members of the Godhead. Each prayer is directed to the Father. Each prayer should be offered pursuant to the power of, and in accordance with, the promptings of the Holy Ghost. Lastly, each prayer should be offered in the name of Jesus Christ.

We Say, "Amen"

As exemplified in the Lord's Prayer (Matt. 6:13), "Amen" is the last word expressed at the end of a prayer. When used by the person offering the prayer, it means "May it be so," or "So be it." Those who hear the prayer and concur in the offering of such a prayer should also repeat aloud the word, "Amen," at the end of the prayer. Such an expression signifies that the hearer of the prayer joins in or approves of the prayer offered.[27]

It is important to listen and pay attention to any prayer given by another in our behalf. When someone else is offering a prayer and we allow our thoughts to drift to other matters, such disrespect and inattentiveness may be considered a vain repetition on our part—a practice the Savior has strongly advised against.[28]

27. D&C 88:135.
28. Matthew 6:7.

5
Prayer Models

Seven Models

Having discussed some of the key elements of an honest, heartfelt prayer, the next step is to review some of the available prayer models from the scriptures. There are many lessons that can be learned from the following seven prayer models:

1. The Lord's Prayer
2. The Joseph Smith Model
3. The Enos Model
4. The Brother of Jared Model
5. The Doctrine and Covenants Section 9 Model
6. Group Prayer
7. The Song of the Righteous

These prayer models provide an opportunity to examine in some detail the prayers offered by the Savior as well as prophets ancient and modern. The purpose of this exercise is to look at their prayer preparation and processes so that we can apply their practices to our prayers. When a particular model is taken from the scriptures, one should first read the complete scriptural passage before reviewing the verses and comments that follow. A prior, overall review of these references will help in discovering greater insights as portions of the scriptures are cited and discussed. Of course, the first model to be examined is the Lord's Prayer.

1. The Lord's Prayer

(Matthew 6:9-13; 3 Nephi 13:9-13)

After this manner therefore pray ye: (Matt. 6:9)

The Savior has commanded us to pray in this fashion. Since the Savior previously directed his followers to avoid vain repetitions in their prayers,[1] his example is the model or format everyone should follow when praying. The instruction Jesus gave to the people in the Americas should be followed today: "As I have prayed among you even so shall ye pray in my church." (3 Nephi 18:16)

Our Father which art in heaven. (Matt. 6:9)

We pray to God, our Father who is in heaven, our creator, the father of our spirits, our Eternal Father. He is a living, divine being, who has a physical body, parts and passions.

Hallowed be thy name. (Matt. 6:9)

The name of God is to be reverenced. One should avoid the unnecessary use and repetition of the name of Deity—a personal commitment to never profane his name. God is addressed in a different form of speech, using words of respect such as *thee, thou* and *thine.*

Thy kingdom come. (Matt. 6:10)

The kingdom of God will one day literally reign on the earth, superior to all other governments and organizations created by man. Knowing this will be so, one commits to consecrate his or her time, energies, talents and all with which they have been blessed to the building up of that kingdom.

Thy will be done in earth, as it is in heaven. (Matt. 6:10)

Notwithstanding the competing tendencies of the natural man, one yields with all one's heart, to do whatsoever God's will for that person may be. With rare exception, people want to learn what God's will is for them, and they want to act in accordance with that will. By saying, "Thy will be done," one is making a promise to be an instrument in God's hand, but only if the person is willing to do what God's hand wants him or her to do. It is a commitment to be totally pliable—his will, not mine, be done.

---

1. "But when ye pray, use not vain repetitions, as the heathen [do]: for they think that they shall be heard for their much speaking." (Matthew 6:7; 3 Nephi 13:7)

Give us this day our daily bread. (Matt. 6:11)

Bread is a basic, life-sustaining food for our mortal bodies. When the physical body is sustained, the opportunity is there to experience the development of one's emotional, intellectual and spiritual "bodies" as well. Acknowledging that we rely on God to provide even the most basic of life's necessities, we recognize that all the other bounties of life are like manna from heaven—sent to bless us as we use those gifts as God intends for them to be used.

And forgive us our debts, as we forgive our debtors. (Matt 6:12)

The principle is simple: A debt is a sin, fault, offense or a trespass. The debtor is a sinner or trespasser. When we forgive others who have wronged or somehow offended us, we will receive Heavenly Father's forgiveness for our trespasses. If we do not forgive others who have wronged or offended us, Heavenly Father will not forgive our sins, faults, offenses or trespasses. We are not being asked to forgive the sin committed by another—we are only being asked to forgive the person who has committed the sin. To the degree that we are liberal in our forgiveness of others, so our Father in Heaven will liberally forgive us. This principle was so important to Jesus that he emphasized its importance immediately following his model for prayer.[2]

And lead us not into temptation, but deliver us from evil. (Matt. 6:13)

Taking the words at their face value, it is tempting to gloss over part of this. It is difficult to understand why anyone would ever pray and ask God not to do something he would never do—he will never lead anyone into temptation. Thanks to the Joseph Smith Translation of this verse, we know that this biblical verse should read, "And suffer us not to be led into temptation. . . ." People should pray for strength to overcome the temptations that they now face or may yet face. The scriptures have promised that no one will be tempted above his or her ability to handle the temptation;[3] consequently, if a

2. Matthew 6:14-15; 3 Nephi 13:14-15; See also Mark 11:24-25.
3. 1 Corinthians 10:13; Alma 13:28.

person wants to be protected from evil, that person must pray for protection and deliverance from such evil.

For thine is the kingdom, and the power, and the glory, for ever. (Matt. 6:13)

There is no tangible reward in this life that can be compared to a blessing from Heavenly Father in the next life. It should be everyone's objective to one day live with Heavenly Father forever. By focusing on the goal of Eternal Life, a person will be more apt to commit to and apply the Christ-like characteristics that he or she has been praying to acquire.

Amen. (Matt 6:13)

Concluding with this word, one offers his "so be it" to the prayer that has just been said. This is a ratification that one gives his commitment to do all that he can to be worthy of the blessings requested.

Considering Jesus' various prayers, John Welch shares some interesting insights:

> Our understanding of Jesus' prayers is heightened by noting that the recorded prayers of Jesus dwell upon three concerns: he thanked God, especially for revealing his word unto the world (Matt. 11:25-27); he continually interceded to seek forgiveness and purification for mankind, even for those who were crucifying him; and he submitted himself to the will of the Father. No better manifestation of these three aspects of the Lord's prayers has been preserved than that which appears in the beautiful nineteenth chapter of 3 Nephi. Here, upon his second appearance to the people of Nephi, Jesus instructed the people to pray, and while they did, he prayed to the Father, saying: "Father, I thank thee that thou hast given the Holy Ghost unto these whom I have chosen; and it is because of their belief in me that I have chosen them out of the world."[4]
>
> Then, after blessing the Nephite people, Jesus turned to pray a second time: "Father, I thank thee that thou hast purified those

---

4. 3 Nephi 19:20.

whom I have chosen . . . that they may be purified in me. . . . that I may be in them as thou, Father, art in me." (3 Nephi 19:28-29)

Finally, Jesus prayed a third time, with words so marvelous that they could not be written. As the result of this prayer, the people were given to know the will of God, receiving miraculous knowledge of him as his will was exercised freely within them. (See 3 Nephi 19:31-34) Jesus' submission to the Father's will characterized his ministry as the Son of God and epitomized his unity with God. In facing his greatest trial, Jesus had prayed, "Not my will, but thine, be done. (Luke 22:42)"[5]

2. The Joseph Smith Model
(Joseph Smith—History)

The Joseph Smith Model is patterned after Joseph Smith's first prayer, a prayer that resulted in the literal appearance of the Father and the Son to the 14-year-old Joseph Smith. For the most part, the formula is simple and self-explanatory. Some of the verses from Joseph Smith's record have been paraphrased below for the purpose of highlighting the key elements of this model.

> ***My mind was called up to serious reflection and great uneasiness; . . . My feelings were deep and often poignant.... In process of time my mind became somewhat partial . . . but . . . it was impossible to come to any certain conclusion. (JS-H 8)***

Evidently, Joseph was mulling many thoughts and concerns through his mind. His meditation or thoughtful reflection tugged at some of his deepest feelings and emotions. As a result of thinking matters through to the best of his own ability, Joseph was inclined to make a certain decision; nevertheless, his mere partiality or tendency toward a particular decision was insufficient to meet the level of certainty he needed to arrive at a conclusion.

> ***While I was laboring under extreme difficulties . . . I was one day reading the Epistle of James. (JS-H 11)***

When the wolves are nipping at a person's heels, is that person inclined to use the scriptures as a resource, whether searching for specific help or just for peace and comfort?

---

5. John W. Welch, "The Lord's Prayers," *Ensign,* Jan. 1976, 15.

So, in accordance with this, my determination to ask of God, I retired to the woods to make the attempt. It was on the morning of a beautiful, clear day. . . . I had never as yet made the attempt to pray vocally. (JS-H 14)

In a previous chapter the blessing of offering a personal prayer in silence—a silent, secret prayer—is mentioned as a unique channel of communication that Satan cannot invade. Joseph was probably unaware of the specific benefits of secret (silent) prayer. There is something of importance to be learned from Joseph's vocal prayer: That there may be grave risks that accompany praying vocally, yet, there are also great rewards that follow vocal, personal prayer. For some, praying out loud helps them focus their thoughts. Some feel their thoughts are less likely to wander while praying out loud.

After I had retired to the place where I had previously designed to go, having looked around me, and finding myself alone, I kneeled down and began to offer up the desires of my heart to God. (JS-H 15)

Are you in a place that is private and secluded? Are you alone? Are you praying with real intent? What does one do when there is a need to pray, but the situation is such that one is neither alone nor in a position that easily permits one to kneel in seclusion? It almost goes without saying that a prayer in one's heart is always helpful, and acceptable. I recall several occasions in the mission field, where my companion and I had to create our own seclusion. We always liked to have a prayer immediately before entering someone's home to present a discussion. On the busy streets of Paris, praying was often difficult to do without drawing undue attention to us. Our method was to put on our dark glasses, unfold a large city map in front of us, with each one holding one side of the map. This allowed us to close our eyes and offer a quiet prayer, while those around us thought we were looking for a street on the map.

Exerting all my powers to call upon God to deliver me . . . At the very moment when I was ready to sink into despair . . . just at this moment of great alarm . . . (JS-H 16)

We must persevere through the very darkest hour of the moment. We must pass through that moment of great alarm, allowing for our hearts, minds and bodies to be wrenched as never before.

My object in going to inquire of the Lord . . . (JS-H 18)

Joseph wanted a confirmation of his inclination to join a particular church—he wanted to know which of all the churches he had frequented was right. There was a purpose in going to the woods to pray. Is there a well-thought-out purpose to our prayers?

> ***Many other things did he say unto me, which I cannot write at this time. . . . I went home. And as I leaned up to the fireplace, mother inquired what the matter was. I replied, "Never mind, all is well—I am well enough off." I then said to my mother, "I have learned for myself . . ." (JS-H 20)***

This is the great lesson of the Joseph Smith model—knowledge. Through prayer, we, too, can learn for ourselves. How is such knowledge made known? The answer comes from the prophet Alma. "Behold, I say unto you they are made known unto me by the Holy Spirit of God. Behold, I have fasted and prayed many days that I might know these things of myself. And now I do know of myself that they are true; for the Lord God hath made them manifest unto me by his Holy Spirit; and this is the spirit of revelation which is in me." (Alma 5:45-46)

> ***There were but few who believed. . . . [I] was ridiculed and reviled. But all this did not destroy the reality of [my] vision. . . . All the persecution under heaven could not make it otherwise. (JS-H 24)***

God's ways are not our ways; consequently, if we act as directed by God, in accordance with what we learned for ourselves, we may be required to suffer mockery, ridicule and even vilification.

> ***They were persecuting me, reviling me, and speaking all manner of evil against me. . . . I was led to say in my heart why does the world think to make me deny what I have actually seen? . . . By so doing I would offend God. . . . (JS-H 25)***

Once a person has embarked on the course known to be God's way, that person will be tempted by the world (those not privy to the things of the Spirit—whether within or without the church) to deny what the person has in reality experienced and knows to be revealed truth. To yield to the world's demands would be like telling one's biological mother that she was not the one who gave you birth.

> ***I continued to pursue my common vocations in life . . . all the time suffering severe persecution . . . both religious and irreligious. . . . (JS-H 27)***

Acting in accordance with revealed truth may bring an unending torrent of severe religious and secular persecution. This is a tremendous challenge for anyone, but especially for a man or woman engaged in trying to earn a living and support a family.

3. The Enos Model (The Book of Enos)

Enos' prayer is notable because of the intense effort Enos put into this recorded prayer. Enos wrestled, struggled and labored in mighty prayer. By pondering these verses, one can almost feel the physical, emotional and spiritual stress experienced by Enos. Once again, some of the verses have been paraphrased, but only for the purpose of highlighting the key elements of this model.

> ***And I will tell you of the wrestle which I had before God . . . And my soul hungered. . . . And while I was thus struggling in the spirit. . . . And it came to pass that after I had prayed and labored with all diligence. . . . (Enos 2, 4, 10, 12)***

It seems that Enos struggled with every fiber of his being. Notwithstanding his extraordinary exertion, the concept of struggling for an answer or blessing from God is not new. The first example in the scriptures comes from the Old Testament. In Genesis 32:24-29, Jacob, seeking a blessing from God, was visited by an angel. There was a literal, physical struggle between Jacob and the angel. Jacob's determination to receive a blessing was so great that he refused to let go of his heavenly messenger until a blessing was given. Through the night, the struggle between these two was so strenuous that Jacob suffered a dislocated hip. The result: Jacob prevailed; a blessing was given.

> ***I kneeled down. (Enos 4)***

Following the Savior's example and directive, when possible and appropriate, we should kneel for our prayers. (3 Nephi 17:13-15)

> ***I cried unto him in mighty prayer and supplication . . . all the day long, and when the night came I did still raise my voice high that it reached the heavens. (Enos 4)***

The blessing of offering personal prayers in silence has been discussed previously. Silent, secret prayer is a channel of communication that Satan cannot invade. As with Joseph Smith, Enos' life was in physical danger, following his vocal prayer. Fortunately, there are also great rewards that follow vocal, personal prayer.

> ***And there came a voice unto me, saying. . . . And while I was thus struggling in the spirit, behold, the voice of the Lord came into my mind again, saying. . . . My faith began to be unshaken in the Lord. I will grant unto thee according to thy desires, because of thy faith. Whatsoever thing ye shall ask in faith believing that ye shall receive in the name of Christ, ye shall receive it. (Enos 5, 10, 11, 12, 15)***

These verses delineate some of the specific blessings that may result from wrestling, hungering, struggling, and laboring in mighty prayer.[6] When it comes to receiving answers to prayers, it cannot get any better than this.

Another excellent example of struggling for an answer to prayer comes from the parable of the unjust judge in the New Testament.[7] In this parable, it appears that a widow had an ongoing complaint against another person, resulting in several court appearances before a certain judge. As is the nature of a parable, the substance of the widow's claim could be any complaint, claim or cause of action anyone may choose to imagine. Although the woman's specific complaint is unknown, some information is provided about the judge. The judge "feared not God, neither regarded man." That phrase tells us that although the judge was not a God-fearing man, he was fair

---

6. See also 3 Nephi 1:11-13.
7. Luke 18:1-8. See Also Matthew 15:21-28; D&C 101:81-88.

and impartial in his treatment of all those who brought their cases before him.

Again, it is unknown whether the widow came before the judge repeatedly because of repeated offenses by her adversary, or whether the matter was trivial and the judge did not feel it was appropriate for her to trouble or annoy the court with such matters. Whatever the circumstances of her complaint, the widow's persistence paid off. Her victory came because she wore down the judge. His patience exhausted, the judge finally decided, or ordered, "Because this widow troubleth me, I will avenge her, lest by her continual coming she weary me." Heavenly Father's role in this parable is summed up with these words in verse eight, "Shall not God avenge his own elect, which cry day and night unto him, though he bear long with them? I tell you that he will avenge them speedily." As with Enos' continuous struggling, the message from this parable is this—Persistent Prayer Pays! Sometimes the victory is an answer to a prayer because we have wearied the Lord into giving us one.

A third example of struggling for an answer to prayer comes, again, from the book of Luke in the New Testament:

> And he said unto them, Which of you shall have a friend, and shall go unto him at midnight, and say unto him, Friend, lend me three loaves; For a friend of mine in his journey is come to me, and I have nothing to set before him? And he from within shall answer and say, Trouble me not: the door is now shut, and my children are with me in bed; I cannot rise and give thee. I say unto you, Though he will not rise and give him, because he is his friend, yet because of his importunity [repeated, insistent knocking and pestering requests] he will rise and give him as many as he needeth. (Luke 11:5-8)

The sleeping man did not get up in the middle of the night and assist his friend because the man was a friend. He got up from his bed, in the middle of the night, to help his friend because the friend's knocking and pounding on his door was annoying and was keeping him awake.

The Enos Model combines elements from each of these referenced scriptures. It is the model wherein persistence, continual prayer, and a physical struggle converge. I have never prayed all day and into the night the way Enos did; nevertheless, I have a first-hand testimony of the principle that persistent prayer pays.

My company decided to move its corporate office from north Michigan to Denver. We needed to sell our home in Michigan so that we could purchase another home in Denver. Since we would be moving in the middle of the school year, timing was critical for our youngest son who was still in high school. As one can imagine, it was also financially critical for our family.

I discussed with my family the principle taught in the parable of the unjust judge. It was my hope that other family members would join me in applying the principle of constant prayer, regarding the single, unrelenting concern of selling our house. Of course, I made the sale of our house an element of every prayer I offered. Whenever I thought about our house or Denver, I offered a prayer. Many times such prayers were quick and silent. I prayed that local real estate brokers would show our home to potential buyers. I prayed that we would receive a fair offer. I prayed that the buyers of our home would be blessed to have their personal affairs fall into place so that they could make an offer on our house. In spite of my persistence, and in spite of how difficult it was to say the words, I regularly prayed that, notwithstanding my selfish desires, God's will would prevail over all else.

I learned that persistent prayer is a funny thing. As I pestered Heavenly Father about the sale of our house, I realized that there are many other concerns in my life that are more important than selling a house. Some of these concerns included the happiness of my children and their families, the success of my children in their schooling, the missionary efforts of my missionary son, the needs of his or her investigators, the efforts of the missionaries throughout the world, the scheduling of a temple visit for a recent member of our branch, the well-being of our nation in the selection of a president, the good health of a sister and the moral cleanliness of a brother. By realizing there were so many other concerns of greater importance, I found it necessary to pray to know about that which I should be praying. I never ceased praying about the sale of our house, but I moved that concern down to a more appropriate place on my priority list.

Yes, we sold our house for a fair price and in a very timely manner. Of the six families that were selling their homes in this corporate move, it would be six months before the next house sold. Thinking about that experience makes me pause and again offer my thanks to God for answering our prayers.

There is one caveat about persistent prayers and wrestling in mighty prayer. If, like a demanding child, a man pesters his Heavenly Father for things or answers that are not in accordance with God's will for him, he may receive the answer he wants; however, he may find himself to be very unhappy. At such a time, the man will find that he sheds more tears over that answered prayer than he would have shed over an unanswered prayer.

4. The Brother of Jared Model
(Ether 2:18-Ether 3:15)

Here is the background for this model. The Lord had visited the brother of Jared on several occasions. On one occasion, the Lord talked with him for a period of three hours, chastening him because he had not remembered to pray. Evidently, the brother of Jared got the message because he repented of the evil he had done.[8] Under the Lord's direction, the brother of Jared, together with his brothers, built some barges in which they were going to cross the ocean. After building the barges as directed, the brother of Jared went to the Lord with three problems: (1) What will we do for light in the barges? (2) How will we steer the barges? (3) How will we get fresh air to keep from suffocating?[9]

The Lord in his generous way provided the answers to questions two and three. The Brother of Jared Model describes how the Lord helped the him arrive at the answer to question number three.

8. Ether 2:14-15.
9. Ether 2:19.

> ***And he cried again unto the Lord. (Ether 2:22)***

We know that a silent, secret prayer is a channel of communication that Satan cannot invade. It is unknown if the brother of Jared was aware of the specific benefits of silent, secret prayer.

> ***I have done even as thou hast commanded me. (Ether 2:22)***

The brother of Jared "checks-in" or reports back on his previous assignment. To his benefit, he reports that he has completed his assigned task in accordance with the will of the Lord.

> ***Behold, there is no light in them. Wilt thou suffer that we shall cross this great water in darkness? (Ether 2:22)***

The specific problem is identified. The brother of Jared asks if traveling in darkness is the will of the Lord.

> ***What will ye that I should do that ye may have light in your vessels? Therefore what will ye that I should prepare for you that ye may have light . . . ? (Ether 22:23-24)***

Having already solved two of the brother of Jared's problems, the Lord keeps the monkey on the right back, asking the brother of Jared what he wants the Lord to do for him. In other words, the Lord asks, "What is your plan?"

> ***The brother of Jared went unto the mount, and did molten out of a rock sixteen small stones. (Ether 3:1)***

Realizing that he had to come up with a plan to find a solution to his problem, the brother of Jared took action—he went to work.

> ***We are unworthy before thee. Thou has given us a commandment that we must call upon thee, that from thee we may receive according to our desires. (Ether 3:2)***

Humbly, the brother of Jared approaches the Lord in prayer, in obedience to the commandment to pray.

> ***I know, O Lord, that thou has all power, and can do whatsoever thou wilt for the benefit of man. (Ether 3:4)***

Humbly, the brother of Jared acknowledges the all-powerful nature of the Lord.

> ***Touch these stones, and they shall shine forth unto us in the vessels, that we may have light. (Ether 3:4)***

The brother of Jared puts his plan into action, making a specific request of the Lord, a request that will be a solution to his problem.

> ***The Lord stretched forth his hand and touched the stones one by one with his finger. (Ether 3-6)***

The Lord grants the brother of Jared's specific request.

> ***Never has man come before me with such exceeding faith as thou hast. For never has man believed in me as thou hast. (Ether 3:9, 3:15)***

Faith plays a major role in receiving an answer to one's prayer. It was a correct principle hundreds of years ago, just as it is a correct principle in our day. In modern scripture, the Lord reveals, "And, as it is written—Whatsoever ye shall ask in faith, being united in prayer according to my command, ye shall receive." (D&C 29:6)

Learning from his dealings with the Lord, thc brother of Jared was very grateful for the blessings given him and his family. He and his family prayed continually, and after their ocean journey and safe arrival, they shed tears of joy because of the multitude of God's tender mercies extended in their behalf.

5. Doctrine and Covenants Section 9 Model

(Doctrine and Covenants Section 9:7-9)

It is possible that this model for prayer may be the best-known but least-understood model among members of The Church of Jesus Christ of Latter-day Saints. It has often been taught that when someone has a decision to make, that person should study the matter out in his own mind, make a decision, then ask God if the decision is right. The exciting element of this model—the part that reaches out and grabs us—is that there is a tangible, physical way for us to receive and recognize a revealed answer. As a signal of the rightness of our decision, the scripture says one will literally receive or feel a burning in the bosom. Additionally, if the decision is wrong, one will experience a stupor of thought that will cause the individual to literally forget the wrong decision. It is appropriate to take a closer look at this model.

You took no thought save it was to ask me. (D&C 9:7)

Oliver Cowdery had not properly prepared for the process of translation. Perhaps he thought some unexplained supernatural process would reveal the proper translation to him.

You must study it out in your mind. (D&C 9:8)

The proper mental exertion must take place. The translator must prayerfully think through the acceptable translation possibilities and then make a decision as to which translation is right.

Then you must ask me if it be right. (D&C 9:8)

The translation that is selected as the right one must be presented to the Lord for confirmation.

> ***If it is right I will cause that your bosom shall burn within you; therefore, you shall feel that it is right. (D&C 9:8)***

If the translator has decided upon the right translation, the Lord will manifest the rightness of the translation by causing his or her bosom to burn.

> ***If it is not right you shall have no such feeling, but you shall have a stupor of thought that shall cause you to forget the thing which is wrong. (D&C 9:9)***

If the translator has decided upon a translation that is not right, there will be no such manifestation; however, the Lord will cause the translator to experience a stupor of thought, resulting in the translator forgetting the wrong translation.

There is a reason that this Section 9 Model is one of the least understood and ill-applied models available to members of the Church. As explained by Elder Jay E. Jensen in a District Conference, this model does not apply to the general decision-making needs we face in our day-to-day lives. This model was given, and is especially tailored, for those engaged in the process of translation. As a consequence, this model has allowed for much frustration, disappointment and confusion among prayerful members of the Church. When applied to non-translation purposes, the physical signals or manifestations may not be received. Consequently, if one follows the general process but does not receive either a burning in the bosom or a stupor of thought, one is left exasperated—wondering, "Why am I not getting an answer to my prayer?"

It is not a suggestion that members cease using these verses as a model for offering their prayers. However, it is suggested that, unless someone is engaged in translation, we should not expect the same manifestations that are promised to those engaged in that process. Elder Bruce R. McConkie of the Quorum of the Twelve Apostles expressed it this way: "We are to solve our own problems and then to counsel with the Lord in prayer and receive a spiritual confirmation that our decisions are correct."[10] From personal experience, I know the manifestations of Section 9 are available to us in response to our prayers. But all should know that they should not always expect such manifestations. In those instances when one does not receive either a burning in the breast or a stupor of thought, one should not conclude that something is wrong with him or her or that the prayer is not being answered.

6. Group Prayers

In 1988, I was looking for employment. During that stressful period, I often asked my children to pray for me to find work. I did this because I felt that they loved me and because I felt that their prayers were more innocent and sincere than mine were. I thought that God might be more inclined to grant their requests than mine. I also felt he possibly might have cause to deny my prayers, but that he could not resist their prayers on my behalf. Matthew records that the Savior instructed his disciples, saying, "If two of you shall agree on earth as touching any thing that they shall ask, it shall be done for them of my Father which is in heaven. For where two or three are gathered together in my name, there am I in the midst of them." (Matt. 18:19-20)

According to Gerald R. Schiefer, when a prayer is offered on behalf of a group,

---

10. Bruce R. McConkie, "Why the Lord Ordained Prayer," *Ensign,* Jan. 1976, 11.

> One person has the responsibility to speak for the group in thanking and asking the Lord's blessing upon them all. This entails being sufficiently humble and in tune with the Spirit that one can receive, through the Holy Ghost, the knowledge of those blessings that would benefit the entire group. Others in the group also have a responsibility to mentally repeat each word and to unite their faith for the same blessings. If this were truly done in each group prayer, we would receive the marvelous promise of the Lord: 'whatsoever ye shall ask in faith, being united in prayer according to my command, ye shall receive.' (D&C 29:6)[11]

Concerning group prayer, I have another personal story to share. For the third time in my career, my employment was being terminated. To get the help I needed, I knew exactly what to do. I consulted with my priesthood quorum leader, asking him if I could address my quorum brethren and ask them for their prayers of support, in order that I might find suitable employment. With my quorum leader's approval, I addressed my priesthood quorum one Sunday morning. I outlined my current situation, then specifically asked that each of them include me in their prayers the following Fast Sunday. I told them that I was doing my part, working diligently to locate a new job opportunity. I asked them to give my request their most serious consideration and remember me in their prayers, so that I would be successful in finding new employment. The result: As faith would have it, before my current job ended, I had located another job that would adequately take care of my employment needs.

I am sure that the combination of fasting and prayer—especially by my quorum brethren—contributed to my finding employment in a timely manner. Yet, the real strength for me came from my faith in the united prayers of my priesthood brethren. Having several times called upon my priesthood quorum to pray for my family's particular needs, I have experienced the blessings available from this type of prayer.

---

11. Gerald R. Schiefer, "Where Two or Three Are Gathered," *Ensign,* Jan. 1976, 35.

There are others who have had a similar successful experience. Consider Trish Pickard of Wichita, Kansas:

> Every day Trish Pickard, 57, helps fight crime in Wichita, Kansas. Her weapon is prayer. "My son and son-in-law are in law enforcement, and when I became aware of the things they deal with, I started to pray for them," she explains. She asks that they be granted physical, emotional, mental and spiritual strength.
>
> Pickard started Citizens Who Care, inviting churches and individuals to adopt officers for daily prayer. What practical effect the organization has on police safety, no one knows. But there's no doubt that the prayers of Citizens Who Care, now 3000 members strong, encourage the officers.
>
> "When you get into a situation where the stress level goes up and the potential for danger increases, you don't have a lot of time to stop and pray for protection," says Lt. John R. Daily of the Sedgwick County Sheriff's Department. "So it's comforting to know that there are people praying for you."[12]

I am a member of a national, professional association related to my field of employment. The Executive Director of that organization sent an e-mail message to the 7,500 association members. The purpose of the message was to inform us that a long-time member of our association was in critical condition in the intensive care unit at a hospital in Dallas, being treated for a sudden and severe case of pneumonia. The Executive Director made this request: "For those so inclined, please pray for his recovery."

Because I was certainly one of those so inclined, I, on several occasions, personally prayed for the recovery and well-being of this association member—a person who, to this day, remains unknown to me. After two weeks, a second e-mail message was broadcast to our association membership. This message stated that our member of concern was finally removed from his ventilator and respirator, was breathing on his own and now communicating with his doctors and family. This good news was accompanied by an expression of

12. Beth J. Lueders, "Clarity," as quoted in *Reader's Digest,* Nov. 2000, 24.

gratitude from our colleague's wife. She was most grateful for the prayerful support from our association members.

Someone once said that there is strength in numbers. When it comes to prayers, there are great blessings available to each of us as a result of the strength of group prayers.

7. Song of the Righteous Model (D&C 25:12)

The last of the prayer models is the song of the righteous. The hymns of the church are marvelous prayers. They give voice to one's thoughts and emotions in powerful ways that a person cannot express with his or her own words. This prayer model comes from the Doctrine and Covenants: "For my soul delighteth in the song of the heart; yea, the song of the righteous is a prayer unto me, and it shall be answered with a blessing upon their heads." (D&C 25:12) The connection between the song of the heart and prayer is most easily identified in the hymns of the church, especially the Sacrament hymns. These hymns serve as a personal prayer that can place almost anyone in a more reverent mood, in preparation for the Sacramental prayers and the partaking of the bread and water.

Various hymns affect people differently, depending upon their use. When used as intended, they serve as personal or group prayers, whether the words are sung out loud or are just followed along silently in one's mind and heart. Try it. Whether out loud or silently to yourself, sing the following hymn and see if you are not filled with a spirit of love for your Eternal Father. Then imagine the power of that spirit as it fills a congregation singing in unison this moving hymn:

"Lord, Accept Our True Devotion"

Lord, accept our true devotion.
Let thy Spirit whisper peace.
Swell our hearts with fond emotion,
And our joy in thee increase.
Never leave us, never leave us.
Help us, Lord, to win the race.
Never leave us, never leave us.
Help us, Lord, to win the race.

Help us all to do thy bidding,
And our daily wants supply.
Give thy Holy Spirit's guiding
Till we reach the goal on high.
Ever guard us, ever guard us,
Till we gain the victory.
Ever guard us, ever guard us,
Till we gain the victory.

May we, with the future dawning,
Day by day rom sin be free,
That on resurrection morning
We may rise at peace with thee,
Ever praising, ever praising,
Thru-out all eternity;
Ever praising, ever praising,
Thru-out all eternity.[13]

Another piece of sacred music that conveys a marvelous message is the hymn, "I Stand All Amazed." In the singing of a congregational hymn of such meaning, the senses of hearing, seeing and feeling are joined in united worship. When the sacred melody and the hymns' poetic verse are combined with the congregational expression of the singers' involved senses, the result can produce a personal manifestation of the Spirit that can only be experienced in a group setting. Again, imagine the prayerful attitude that accompanies this hymn:

"I Stand All Amazed"

I stand all amazed at the love Jesus offers me,
Confused at the grace that so fully he proffers me.
I tremble to know that for me he was crucified,
That for me, a sinner, he suffered he bled and died.

13. "Lord, Accept Our True Devotion," *Hymns,* The Church of Jesus Christ of Latter-day Saints, no. 107.

I marvel that he would descend from his throne divine
To rescue a soul so rebellious and proud as mine,
That he should extend his great love unto such as I,
Sufficient to own, to redeem and to justify.

I think of his hands pierced and bleeding to pay the debt!
Such mercy, such love, and devotion can I forget?
No, no, I will praise and adore at the mercy seat,
Until at the glorified throne I kneel at his feet.

Oh it is wonderful that he should care for me
Enough to die for me!
Oh, it is wonderful, wonderful to me![14]

Elder Merrill J. Bateman of the Seventy tells a story about a handicapped young woman whose favorite song truly was a prayer to God:

> This story concerns a young girl, the fourth child in a family of six children. Her name is Heather. Three of the children, including Heather, suffered from a rare disease called glutaric acidemia. In each case, the onset of the disease occurred during the first year of life when an enzyme attacked the brain, causing paralysis. The disease results in acid forming in the muscles similar to that which occurs following a period of intense physical activity. The problem faced by the children was that the acid never leaves and causes great pain. Cindy, the first child with the disease, died at the age of 23. She was one of the oldest living persons known with the disease. At death she weighed about 40 pounds. Soon after Heather's birth, the parents realized that she would be physically handicapped and that her spirit would be housed in a body with great restrictions. As she grew, she was confined to a wheelchair, was unable to speak, and could send messages only with her eyes. A direct gaze and a smile meant

14. "I Stand All Amazed," *Hymns,* The Church of Jesus Christ of Latter-day Saints, no. 193.

yes. A blink meant no. Despite the handicaps, one could feel her vibrant spirit.

As Heather progressed, it became obvious to her parents that she was extraordinarily bright. She would play guessing games with the family using her limited means to communicate. When she was old enough, the parents enrolled Heather in a special school to see if she could learn to speak. The teacher was a gifted therapist. One morning as Heather and the teacher visited about the prior weekend, the teacher learned that Heather had attended Primary. The teacher then sang for Heather "When He Comes Again."

The expression on Heather's face revealed the delight within her. When the teacher asked Heather if she had a favorite song, the young girl's wide eyes and engaging smile left little doubt. But what was the song? Through a series of questions, the teacher learned that Heather's song was one she had heard in Primary. She wasn't sure which songbook it was in, but it was about Jesus. The teacher sang all the songs she could think of, but to no avail. However, Heather was not about to quit; she wanted to share her favorite song. At the end of the day, the two were still searching. The teacher agreed to bring her songbooks to school the next day.

On the following morning, Heather and her teacher continued the quest. From the first hymn to the last, the little girl blinked her eyes, indicating no. They were still unsuccessful. Finally, the teacher told Heather that her mother would have to help her find the song and then they would sing it.

The next day Heather arrived with the green Church hymnal tucked in her chair, but there was no marker. So they began with the first hymn. The teacher would sing the first part of each song, and Heather would give her answer. After the first 100 hymns, there were 100 no's. After 200 hymns there had been 200 no's. Finally, the teacher began to sing, "There is sunshine in my soul today." Heather's body jumped, and a big smile crossed her face. Her eyes gazed directly into the teacher's, indicating success after three days of searching. Both teacher and student rejoiced.

As the teacher sang the first verse and began the chorus, Heather mustered all her strength and joined in with a few sounds. After finishing the first verse and chorus, the teacher asked if she wanted to hear the rest of the verses, and Heather's eyes opened wide with a firm yes. The teacher began to sing:

There is music in my soul today,
A carol to my King,
And Jesus listening can hear
The songs I cannot sing.

Heather's reaction to these lines was so strong that the teacher stopped. As the reality and significance of the words pressed on the teacher's mind, she asked: "Heather, is that what you like about the song? Is that what you want me to know? Does Jesus listen? Does He hear the songs you cannot sing?"

The direct, penetrating gaze indicated yes.

Feeling guided by the Spirit, the teacher asked, "Heather, does Jesus talk to you in your mind and in your heart?"

Again, the child's look was penetrating.

The teacher then asked, "Heather, what does He say?"

The teacher's heart pounded as she saw the clear look in Heather's eyes as the little girl awaited the questions that would allow her to share her insights.

"Does Jesus say, 'Heather, I love you'?"

Heather's radiant eyes widened, and she smiled.

After a pause, the teacher asked next, "Does He say, 'Heather, you're special'?"

The answer again was yes.

Finally the teacher asked, "Does He say, 'Heather, be patient; I have great things in store for you'?"

Heather summoned all her strength, and her head became erect and her eyes penetrated the teacher's soul. She knew she was loved, she was special, and she needed only to be patient.

Two years later, Heather died because of the ravages of the disease. Her younger brother Mark also suffers from the disease but not to the extent of his older sisters. He can talk, although it is not easy. As the parents discussed Heather's passing and the funeral that would take place, Mark exclaimed, "No go Heather's funeral!" Heather was his best friend. As the parents tried to explain death to him, he would not be consoled. He was crushed and did not want to attend the service. For two days he could not be persuaded.

On the morning of the funeral, the father went to Mark's room to get him up. As he entered the room, Mark was sitting up in bed with a big smile on his face. His first words were, "Dad, go Heather's funeral!"

The father responded, "Mark, what has changed your mind?"

"Dad, had dream."

"What did you dream about, Mark?"

"Dad, dreamed about Heather."

"Mark, what was Heather doing?"

"Oh, Dad, Heather running and jumping and singing, 'There is sunshine in my soul today.' Dad, go Heather's funeral."

May we rejoice in the power of sacred hymns to lift our souls and to bear testimony. Truly "the song of the righteous is a prayer unto [God], and it shall be answered with a blessing upon [our] heads" (D&C 25:12).[15]

---

15. Merrill J. Bateman, "The Power of Hymns," *Ensign,* Jul. 2001, 15.

6

Personal Revelation—I Have Learned for Myself

The Perfect Reply

An excellent foundation has now been formed in preparation for receiving discernable answers to prayers. *First,* there is the knowledge that God lives and that there is an answer for every prayer. *Second,* there is a daily effort to develop the character and attributes of a seeker of truth and light. *Third,* an effort is being made to prepare properly for prayers. *Fourth,* there is the application of the specific key elements of a proper prayer. *Fifth,* the scriptures have been searched and pondered, including the prayer methods and models as provided by the Savior and the prophets.

Now what? What comes next is one of the most exciting aspects of the restored gospel—learning to recognize the revealed will of the Lord that is always provided in answer to prayer. In learning to recognize such answers to prayer, one will also learn to accept that answer in whatever manner, form and time Heavenly Father chooses to make it known.

For many years, it has been the desire of some that the answers to their prayers be so discernable that they unmistakably know the answer is from God and that they understand the answer clearly. Such individuals have a strong conviction that they can deal with the answer, whatever it may be—they only want the answer to be discernable. These people neither ask for, nor require, a visit from a heavenly messenger to tell them the most effective way to teach a Sunday School class. Likewise, they do not need a grand manifestation to make known what they should do to discipline their teenage child. What will satisfy the desires of their hearts and fill their souls with joy will be a still small voice, a feeling of peace in their hearts or a gentle nudge—recognized by them to be from their Heavenly Father. It absolutely does not matter what the answer is. Knowing in their own minds and hearts that the answer is from God, not from their own thoughts or some deceiving source, is a blessing beyond these individuals' ability to describe in words.

Most men and women do not understand the laws of nature, physics or heaven; consequently, they cannot explain how communications occur between themselves, as mortals, and their Heavenly Father. Neither do these people understand the process by which revelation is provided. Without having to be explained, it is as if there is something in their spiritual character—a part of their spirit's DNA—that permits them, during their mortal existence, to receive communications from the Father, Son and Holy Ghost, inhibited only by an offensive attitude or their inappropriate or poor choices. These men and women know, however, that revelation is more spiritual in its manifestations than physical.

President Joseph F. Smith has observed, "The Spirit of God speaks to our spirits. The Lord does not communicate to us very often through our natural senses, but when He speaks He speaks to the immortal part; the spirit of man receives the communications the Lord sends to His children, and we must therefore be in harmony to receive them."[1] Because most people do not thoroughly understand the process of spiritual communication, and because they are more tied into the physical rather than the spiritual world (and probably more so for men than women), they will often receive revelation or otherwise be worked upon by the Spirit without realizing it.

I found this spiritual-physical distinction to be most obvious when I served as a Bishop. It was almost always after the occurrence of a very simple experience that I realized I had been a part of the revelatory process. One Sunday afternoon following our block meetings, I interviewed a young man in my ward—it was his annual Aaronic Priesthood interview with the bishop. The interview went smoothly—detailed questions were asked, direct answers were

---

1. Joseph F. Smith, "Discourse by President Joseph F. Smith," *Millenial Star,* 6 Sep. 1906, 561-62. Also, Priesthood Manual, *Teachings of Presidents of the Church: Joseph F. Smith,* 202-203.

given. Yet, at the end of the interview, I suspected that this young man had not told me the complete truth. The following Sunday, this young man's mother stopped me in the hallway at church. She stated, "I don't know what you said to my son last week, but whatever it was, he says you are definitely inspired." I scrunched up furrows on my forehead as I tried to recall my interview with her son. As I replayed the interview in my mind, I recalled, without commenting to the mother, that as I concluded the visit with her son, I said something to him like this, "Something tells me you have not been completely honest with me during this interview." There was this very uncomfortable pause and no additional words were spoken as the young man silently left my office. For me, it was an experience that seemed almost routine, yet was actually an answer to my many prayers to know what to do and what to say as I fulfilled the calling as Bishop.

Rachelle, a young mother of two boys, relates an experience regarding such spiritual matters. She and her family were living in a small town in northern Arizona. Rachelle was taking classes to become certified as a member of the ski patrol at a mountain ski resort some miles away. As part of her program, she was required to drive to another town to take part in training from time to time.

For Rachelle, this day began like so many others. Like most busy moms, she often prayed each day that her family would be safe through the day and that Heavenly Father would guide her actions. In the morning as she prepared to leave home for a day of training on the slopes, Rachelle had a few thoughts that perhaps she should not go. Such thoughts were easily dismissed because she had made the necessary arrangements, including a babysitter for her boys. After dropping her boys at the sitter's house, Rachelle drove out of town. After driving only a few miles, the thoughts returned, nudging her not to go, but to return home. She pulled her car to the side of the road, to think and recalibrate, in hopes of making some sense of the thoughts and feelings she was having.

Rachelle decided to turn around and head home to see if that would make her feel better. As she headed back to the sitter's house, she did not feel any more at peace than before she turned around to head home. So, Rachelle turned back around and headed back out of town toward the mountain resort. This time, the foreboding feelings seemed much heavier than before. Rachelle gave up on the notion of practicing that day and returned to the sitter's house and picked up her boys.

When at home, she put her eighteen-month-old son in the highchair for a snack. Suddenly, the little boy went into a seizure. His face took on a frozen look of anger, then a look of terror. His face turned blue, and his body stiffened, while his arms and hands curled into his chest. Rachelle pulled the boy from his highchair. As the toddler's breathing stopped, Rachelle prepared to perform her recently acquired knowledge of CPR. She started to lay him down to perform CPR, when he let out a little whimper, telling her he was breathing once again.

As her little son seemed to return to a state of physical normalcy, Rachelle held him in her arms while she sobbed and he slept. Rachelle consulted medical authorities, and learned that her son had experienced a reaction to a recent DPT vaccine. Rachelle was most grateful that she listened to the Spirit's promptings to return home, so that she could be there for her son during those moments of crisis. It is unknown what might have happened if Rachelle had not been there. Rachelle learned from that experience the unique way Heavenly Father communicates his will to her, as well as the importance of yielding to Heavenly Father's will rather than to her personal plans.

Even though it may not be possible to explain how divine communication works, one should not be concerned how prayers and answers are processed and effected through the Father, Son and Holy Ghost. In like fashion, people should not be concerned whether the answer to a prayer comes from the Father, Son or Holy Ghost. When an answer comes directly from any one member of the Godhead, it may be treated just as if the answer came directly from either one of the others. It is impossible for any member of the Godhead to provide a better or more appropriate answer to a prayer than one of the other members of the Godhead can provide. In some indescribable manner, the members of the Godhead unite to provide the perfect, discernable reply to our prayers. There is no other way it can be done. The important point to understand about this concept is this: answers to a prayer may come in stages, in different ways at different times and from or through different members of the Godhead; nevertheless, the answers we receive will always be in perfect sequence, content and method of delivery.

There Is an Answer to Every Prayer

Let the declaration once again resound: there is an answer to every sincere prayer. Everyone that asks receives an answer. It is a basic doctrine taught in the scriptures. The modern scriptures teach, "Verily, verily, I say unto thee, blessed art thou for what thou hast done; for thou has inquired of me, and behold as often as thou hast inquired thou hast received instruction of my Spirit." (D&C 6:14) Notwithstanding this basic teaching, it must be kept in mind that the purpose of one's prayers is not to assist as if it were Aladdin's lamp. Similarly, prayer is not a vending machine where one deposits a few coins and receives a particular item or answer of choice.

Perhaps reflecting in part on the teaching of President Brigham Young, Bruce R. McConkie addresses this topic:

> It is not, never has been, and never will be the design and purpose of the Lord—however much we seek him in prayer—to answer all our problems and concerns without some effort or struggle on our part. This mortality is a probationary estate. In it we have our agency. We are being tested to see how we will respond in various situations; how we will decide issues; what course we will pursue while we are here walking, not by sight, but by faith. Hence, we are to solve our own problems and then to counsel with the Lord in prayer and receive a spiritual confirmation that our decisions are correct.[2]

---

2. Bruce R. McConkie, "Why the Lord Ordained Prayer," *Ensign,* Jan. 1976, 7. President Brigham Young also addressed this point when he stated, "If I ask him to give me wisdom concerning any requirement in life, or in regard to my own course, or that of my friends, my family, my children, or those that I preside over, and get no answer from him, and then do the very best that my judgment will teach me, he is bound to own and honor that transaction, and he will do so to all intents and purposes." (*Journal of Discourses,* Vol. 3, 205)

While the basic principle is that there is an answer to every prayer, nowhere in the scriptures is it taught that such an answer will come without some or even great effort, struggle, faith, labor or difficulty.

Elder Richard G. Scott has taught us,

> When we explain a problem and a proposed solution, sometimes He answers yes, sometimes no. Often He withholds an answer, not for lack of concern, but because he loves us—perfectly. He wants us to apply truths He has given us. For us to grow, we need to trust our ability to make correct decisions. We need to do what we *feel* is right. In time, He will answer. He will not fail us.
>
> When He answers *yes,* it is to give us confidence.
>
> When He answers *no,* it is to prevent error.
>
> When He *withholds an answer,* it is to have us grow through faith in Him, obedience to His commandments, and a willingness to act on truth. We are expected to assume accountability by acting on a decision that is consistent with His teachings without prior confirmation. We are not to sit passively waiting or to murmur because the Lord has not spoken. We are to act.[3]

Relying on one's personal efforts and making one's own decisions makes receiving discernable answers to prayers much like farming. One must till, plant, weed, water, fertilize and constantly tend to the land, day-in and day-out, year round, in order to enjoy a bounteous harvest. Similarly, each person must constantly work to develop faith that God lives. Everyone must make the daily effort to develop the character and attributes of a seeker of revelation. Each person should prepare for his or her prayers. Everyone should apply the key elements of a proper prayer. All should search the scriptures and ponder the prayer methods and models as provided by the Savior and the prophets. Everyone should be prepared for revelation.

When one is prepared for revelation, that person will be willing to wait and listen for the answer, recognize it when it comes, and act on the Lord's counsel when it is given. When it comes, it will flow

---

3. Richard G. Scott, *General Conference Report,* "Learning to Recognize Answers to Prayer," *Ensign,* Nov. 1989, 31.

in only one direction—from God to that person. The answers will be varied and many. The prophet Alma mentions some of the various ways prayers may be answered: "After having had all things made known unto them, according to their desires, and their faith, and prayers, of that which has been, and which is, and which is to come; Having been visited by the Spirit of God; having conversed with angels, and having been spoken unto by the voice of the Lord; and having the spirit of prophecy, and the spirit of revelation, and also many gifts, the gift of speaking with tongues, and the gift of preaching, and the gift of the Holy Ghost, and the gift of translation." (Alma 9:20-21)

The means used by God to answer prayers are many. A voice may come to a man's mind. The Spirit may utter peace to a woman's heart. One's bosom may burn. A person may be led or constrained. The Spirit may press upon a boy or girl's feelings. No matter how the answer comes, if one is prepared, it will be discernable. Receiving a discernable answer to one's prayers will be a blessing beyond a person's ability to describe in words.

As an individual examines the various ways prayers may be answered, that person will most likely discover that he or she is more inclined or susceptible to certain types of answers than to others. James E. Talmage taught this very concept. He states that, "The directness and plainness with which God may communicate with man is dependent upon the conditions of receptivity of the person. One may be susceptible to inspiration in its lower and simpler phases only; another may be so thoroughly responsive to this power as to be capable of receiving direct revelation; and this higher influence again may manifest itself in varying degrees, and with a greater or lesser shrouding of the divine personality."[4]

Having a particular sensitivity to the promptings of the Spirit or strength in one area may mean that some people may never experience certain kinds of answers—and that is reasonable. Since everyone's objective is to learn to receive discernable answers, the method by which it comes is of little consequence. Of great conse-

---

4. James E. Talmage, *Articles of Faith,* Salt Lake City: The Church of Jesus Christ of Latter-day Saints, 1947, 297.

quence is the person's ability to recognize the answer as it is revealed. As one seeks to recognize the answers, one should keep in mind the counsel provided by L. Lionel Kendrick:

> In the economy of heaven the Lord never uses a floodlight when a flashlight is sufficient—and so it is in receiving personal revelation. This principle is true even with revelation that comes to prophets. President Kimball once said: "The great volume of revelation . . . come[s] to today's prophets in the less spectacular way—that of deep impressions, but without spectacle or glamour or dramatic events accompanying. Expecting the spectacular, one may not be fully alerted to the constant flow of revealed communication."[5]

Just as day-to-day discernable answers will come without fanfare, one may also find that a new or different answer may not be given under those circumstances where the answer has been provided previously. Such previous, specific insight or instruction may be already given in the scriptures, General Conference talks, personal patriarchal blessings or in previous direct counsel given by local church leaders.

Does it matter how the answer comes, so long as the answer comes with clarity? No. Clarity should be sought in the substance of the answer rather than in the spectacle of the form of the answer. Now is the time to examine the various discernable ways prayers may be answered.

The Scriptures

The scriptures are a great source of personal revelation. Joseph Smith's experience with the scriptures is a perfect example of the impact reading, studying and pondering the scriptures can have on us. Sincere concerns about religion occupied the fourteen-year-old mind of Joseph Smith. After reading in the Bible, James 1:5, he said, "Never did any passage of scripture come with more power to the heart of man than this did at this time to mine. It seemed to enter

5. L. Lionel Kendrick, "Personal Revelation," *Ensign,* Sep. 1999, 10.

with great force into every feeling of my heart." (Joseph Smith—History 1:12) As it happened with Joseph Smith, so it may happen to anyone else who reads the scriptures. While studying and searching the scriptures, a certain passage may have a dramatic impact on the reader. The passages may appear almost illuminated as they are read. Answers to prayers may come as the Lord speaks to the reader through the scriptures. This is possible because of the promise that "the words of Christ will tell you all things what ye should do." (2 Nephi 32:3) Part of the power of the scriptures is that they are always immediately available when inspiration is needed. Brother Bassett's insights on this subject are helpful:

> When we seek the guidance of the Lord, it is wise to start first with what the Lord has already had to say about life through others who have talked with him. Scripture study and the words of living oracles of God provide a good starting point for meditation. We seek the voice of God in prayer; we also seek the voice of God in the scriptures. The two are simply different facets of a common quest; each enhances the other, each is vital to the function of the other. In the main, scripture emphasizes what the Lord has had to say to the Church or to the world in general; prayer emphasizes what the Lord has to say to us in particular.
>
> Contemplation of the messages found in the scriptures often provides a good preface to prayer. The Prophet Joseph was led to the Sacred Grove in response to the words of James and to the waters of the Susquehanna and baptism by prophets of the Book of Mormon. We too may receive spiritual promptings from what prophets—past and present—have had to say.
>
> Scripture reading draws us away from the world into the realm of the things of God and supplies a focal point for our meditation, a seed, as it were, for the flowering of personal revelation. It provides yet another channel through which the Lord may speak to us—or at least begin the process of speaking to us. Coupled with the other facets of the prayer process mentioned above, it can open new vistas in our lives.[6]

Richard G. Scott of the Quorum of the Twelve Apostles also describes a method of using the scriptures to receive revelation:

---

6. Arthur R. Bassett, "Before Praying," *Ensign,* Jan. 1976, 31.

"Answers can come through reading the scriptures. Read, ponder and pray about the meaning of specific verses. Analyze and unite related scriptures. Then prepare a statement of principle that embodies the truths contained in these scriptures. When this is done, you can be instructed through inspiration as you search the scriptures."[7]

Members of the Church believe that God's words have been revealed, many of which are found the scriptures. The scriptures, however, do not address every concern or issue about which one requires guidance on a daily basis. That is why Heavenly Father's words are currently revealed and will continually be revealed to boys, girls, mothers, fathers and Church leaders. The scriptures alone are not enough. Everyone that is striving daily to cope with the challenges of a rapidly changing world requires continuous personal revelation beyond that which is provided in the published scriptures.

Follow Your Leaders

The Saturday evening Priesthood Session of General Conference in 1987 will always be a memorable one for me. It was one of those trying periods of my life when I was out of work. President Thomas S. Monson counseled us in that meeting to be more generous in the giving of our fast offerings—to double our contribution if possible. He may have actually been speaking to the Church's worldwide priesthood body, but I felt like he was speaking only to me. He quoted President Marion G. Romney, saying, "If we will double our fast offerings, we shall increase our own prosperity, both spiritually and temporally. This the Lord has promised, and this has been the record."[8] No greater financial advice had come to the heart of man than that counsel had at that time to mine. I knew what I would do to find work—I would follow President Monson's counsel. It is difficult to put my feelings into words. I felt sorry for myself, yet felt blessed because I still had money in the bank, still had my house and, above all, still had a wife and family that loved and stood by me. It was as if I had discovered the formula, personal to me, to extricate myself from the mire of unemployment.

---

7. Richard G. Scott, CES Symposium, BYU, 1998.

8. Thomas S. Monson, *General Conference Report,* "Goal Beyond Victory," *Ensign,* Nov. 1988, 45.

When I returned home, I was spiritually filled. As I walked through the kitchen, my wife asked, "How was the meeting?" I was so emotionally choked up I felt like bursting into tears. It seemed as if I barely squeaked out the words, "We need to double our fast offering."

The next week at Church, we made a fast offering contribution that was twice as much as the normal fast offering we had been paying. Then they began to happen—little events of consequence. Coincidences took on the label of small, miraculous events. I soon received and accepted a full-time job offer. Before the month of October was over, I had returned to full-time employment at a salary sufficient to take care of my family's financial needs. Oh, what gratitude filled my heart and prayers.

Unbelievably, two years later it happened again. Almost 40 percent of my company was laid off, leaving me, for the second time, without full-time employment. Maybe it goes without saying, but I was shocked to find myself in this familiar, but terrible, predicament—it was embarrassing and humiliating to go through such an experience so soon after my first adventure of unemployment.

Unemployment can be a very depressing period of a man's life. My prayers, once again, went into a pleading mode. I pleaded that I would not be angry with God, that I would understand the purpose for such a repeat experience, that I would have the wherewithal to handle the moment and succeed at finding full-time employment. I prayed for forgiveness for whatever I may have thought or done to have to suffer through this painful process again.

After six months of diligent, but unsuccessful job-hunting, I attended our Stake Conference where Elder Robert L. Backman was the presiding authority. In the Saturday afternoon Priesthood training session, he taught us in-depth about quorum brotherhood. I took his specific instruction to heart and implemented it. At the time, I was serving as the Bishop of our ward and needed the strength and support of my High Priests Group. More than anything, I wanted their spiritual support to help me in my job search.

The week prior to Fast Sunday, my High Priests Group Leader allowed me to talk to the priesthood brethren of my quorum. I shared with them my employment needs, my job-hunting efforts up to that time and my request for their prayers and support. I asked my quorum brethren, and friends, if they would consider making me a part of their prayers as they fasted the next Sunday. On that Fast Sunday, once again with the support of my High Priests Group Leader, I addressed my quorum. I thanked them for their support and for including me in their prayers. I made only one request, which was that if they had unintentionally forgotten to think of me as they prayed that day, that they would please do so.

As I excused myself from the quorum meeting to join the priests quorum, one of my quorum brothers grabbed my arm. He suggested that I speak with another brother in our ward, our Elders Quorum President. I made an appointment to meet the Elders Quorum President at his place of business the next Saturday morning. Since he was "coincidentally" looking for someone to fill a need in his business organization, he offered me a position with his company. How could we not have been an answer to each other's prayers?

I am so glad I followed the counsel of the Church leader visiting our stake conference. I have a testimony that the Lord answers our prayers through his chosen leaders. This simple principle was taught by the Savior when he said, "What I the Lord have spoken, I have spoken, . . . whether by mine own voice or by the voice of my servants, it is the same." (D&C 1:38)

Feelings of the Heart

One of the ways personal revelation is received is through feelings received in the heart. It is very common that such feelings are experienced at the same time that thoughts come to the mind; however, for the moment, the focus is the feelings of, and impressions upon, the heart.

In recognizing that feelings are one of the ways people receive answers to their prayers, one of the challenges that is faced is giving proper meaning to the feelings that are received in the heart. Elder Boyd K. Packer has taught that men and women's emotional and spiritual sensitivities are very closely linked; consequently, it is possible to mistake an emotional impression for something spiritual. As a result, some people may receive what they believe to be spiritual promptings from God when such promptings are derived from one's emotions or from the adversary. Promptings derived from one's own emotions or originating from the adversary can be counterfeits for the Spirit. Evidently, such counterfeit messages must not be uncommon, otherwise Elder Packer would not have advised us to always be "on guard lest you be deceived by inspiration from an unworthy source."[9] When such counterfeit feelings originate with the adversary, they are carefully crafted for the sole purpose of deceiving us into thinking they are promptings or impressions from the Spirit.

In a speech at Brigham Young University, Sally Taylor commented on the distinction between the spirit and personal emotion:

> At times I have thought a feeling of excitement was the Spirit speaking, but I discovered that I was wrong. The voice of the Spirit isn't an excitement buzz. I have found that there is positive excitement and negative excitement. When a positive exciting thing comes—like the birth of a grandchild—with it also comes a deep joy and a spirit of peace. That accompanying joy and peace is not there in the negative excitement. Mob reactions create an electricity that is exciting. Defying the law by robbing, stealing, doing drugs, vandalizing and even killing are reported to create an exciting high. Excitement in and of itself is not the Holy Ghost creating a feeling in our hearts.[10]

The important distinction between impressions of the Spirit and non-spiritual emotional feelings were also a concern of President Howard W. Hunter. He addressed this delicate matter in the following way:

> I get concerned when it appears that strong emotion or free-flowing tears are equated with the presence of the Spirit. Certainly the Spirit of the Lord can bring strong emotional feelings, including tears, but that outward manifestation ought not to be confused with the presence of the Spirit itself.

---

9. Boyd K. Packer, "The Candle of the Lord," *Ensign,* Jan. 1983, 55.
10. Sally Taylor, *Speeches,* "The Holy Ghost: Our Infallible Guide," BYU Devotional Address, 5 Nov. 1996.

> I have watched a great many of my brethren over the years and we have shared some rare and unspeakable spiritual experiences together. Those experiences have all been different, each special in its own way, and such sacred moments may or may not be accompanied by tears. Very often they are, but sometimes they are accompanied by total silence. Other times they are accompanied by joy. Always they are accompanied by a great manifestation of the truth, of revelation to the heart. . . .
>
> Listen for the truth, hearken to the doctrine, and let the manifestation of the Spirit come as it may in all of its many and varied forms.[11]

One cannot over-emphasize the importance of the feelings in the heart as a person discerns the answers to his or her prayers. The natural eyes will see many marvelous things; however, most have learned that seeing is not necessarily believing, because things are not always as they appear. One may also hear many things, but what a person hears may not be all there is to hear; consequently, what we hear may be true, but it may not be the whole truth. The natural senses are subject to deception; however, personal revelation to the heart will never deceive.

President Joseph F. Smith addressed this subject in the following manner by stating:

> But let me tell you when the Almighty reveals Himself unto man, He does it by the power of the Holy Ghost, and not through the natural eye or the natural ear. He speaks to man as if He were speaking to him independent of his body; He speaks to the spirit. Therefore, if God Almighty speaks to you and bears record of His truth by the power of the Holy Ghost, . . . you will know as God knows. It will not be something that you believe only; something that has been communicated to you through your natural senses, in which you may be mistaken or deceived; but it will be that which God has spoken to the heart, to the living soul, to the eternal being of man, which, like God, is indestructible and eternal.[12]

---

11. President Howard W. Hunter, as quoted in *Teaching, No Greater Call,* Salt Lake City: The Church of Jesus Christ of Latter-day Saints, 1978, 47.

12. *Teachings of Presidents of the Church: Joseph F. Smith,* The Church of Jesus Christ of Latter-day Saints, Salt Lake City, 1998, 6.

The Holy Ghost will neither fill our hearts with anger, fear or contention, nor offer a harsh motivation to act. Such feelings are the unique traits of Satan and his angels of darkness. The voice of the Holy Ghost is a voice of gentle motivation to stimulate action. The types of feelings we can receive are love, joy, peace, longsuffering, gentleness, goodness, faith, meekness, hope, confidence and temperance.[13] These kinds of feelings cannot be experienced in one's mind, yet they can fill the heart. Thus, when the heart can tell someone something that the mind does not or cannot tell that individual, that person is receiving the Spirit of the Lord.[14] We are receiving truth and light without the ability to confirm or process it through one of our natural senses.

For the most part, such discernable answers through feelings of the heart will come in response to questions typically calling for a "yes" or "no" answer, such as: Is this the right job for me at this time? Is the church really true? Should I accept this church calling? Is now the time for me to submit my mission papers? Will my family and I be able to weather this financial crisis? Is this what thou would have me do? Should I apologize to my daughter?

Typically, when the answer is in the affirmative, the good feelings mentioned above are communicated as a positive, identifiable feeling in one's heart. On the other hand, when the answer is in the negative, there is no such positive feeling. In fact, there is either a negative feeling or it feels negative because the Spirit has made it very discernable by the obvious absence of any positive feeling.

Personally, I have a much easier time recognizing negative feelings associated with a negative answer or the making of a wrong decision. I find such communications very clear. My mind says, "Yes, your plan of action is sound and makes sense," but my heart tells me, "Positively not! Absolutely no way!"

Here is an example. A playwright in our city felt impressed to ask my wife and me to be the two main characters in his play about the Book of Mormon on trial. I was intrigued by the opportunity to take on the challenge of a major acting role and selfish enough to enjoy

---

13. Galatians 5:22-23; John 14:27.

14. Harold B. Lee, "Personal Revelation," *Ensign,* Sep. 1999, 11.

the chance at some publicity and recognition. I thought the script was well done and that my wife and I could master the parts and properly fulfill the roles. However, over a period of days, even though I envisioned stardom in my mind, I began to feel overall gloomy about the opportunity.

This gloomy feeling lingered for several days. It is a characteristic of this type of answer that the feeling lingers—it dwells in the heart.[15] The feeling was not fleeting—it constantly gnawed at my emotions and overpowered my rational thoughts. Having learned to respect this feeling when "things" are not right, my wife and I turned down the acting opportunity.

I immediately felt at peace. I was no more dragged down by that intangible, gloomy force. Within one week of turning down the parts, we received a telephone call from our son who was across the world, serving a full-time mission. Due to an illness, he would be returning home within days—a month earlier than planned—so that he could get the medical attention he needed. Immediately upon his return and throughout his recovery process, our son needed a great deal of our physical and emotional attention that we could not have given in sufficient quantities if we had committed to develop our acting talents and participate in the "fame and fortune" of the stage.

Individuals can also learn to recognize the feelings they are having as answers to their prayers when such feelings are attended by deep feelings of love and concern for their families, friends, neighbors and communities.[16] This does not necessarily mean that the feeling of love for families and friends is the answer. It means that such feelings are indicative that such individuals are in the proper spiritual frame of mind to receive other promptings or feelings.

I remember one day petitioning my Heavenly Father to help me escape a significant financial hardship. I was filled with doubt, loneliness and fear. Seeking privacy, I went downstairs to the basement family room to pray. I recorded this story in my journal; however, the focus of the journal entry centered on one of my sons. As I knelt

15. D&C 8:2.
16. Enos 1:9; Alma 6:6, 34:27.

down to pray, I could hear my five-year-old son, Jon, playing in one of the nearby basement window wells. I listened to his little-boy chatter as he played by himself.

As I prayed, I did not know if my particular financial affliction would be lifted, but I did know that I loved Jonnie and that likewise my dad loved me. I was filled with an overwhelming feeling of love for my children, desiring nothing but the best for them, at the same time hoping that my Heavenly Father loved me as much, and desired nothing but the best for me. My journal entry from that night also reflects the feelings I had after my prayer. I recorded, "I feel afraid—that I really can't have it [financial relief] even if I want it. I now must trust others. I must have faith and trust my Heavenly Father."

One of the ways the Spirit may reveal the will of the Lord to a person is through the feelings of the heart. It is the individual's responsibility to be sensitive to those feelings. It is important that every person accept the responsibility to be sensitive to such feelings in the heart because the Lord has promised, "I will tell you in your . . . heart, by the Holy Ghost, which shall come upon you. . . ." (D&C 8:2)

The Spirit Speaks Peace to our Minds

One of the oldest and most familiar ways the Lord speaks to man and answers his prayers is by speaking peace to his mind.[17] Once again, the scriptures provide the instruction regarding this concept: "Verily, verily, I say unto you, if you desire a further witness, cast your mind upon the night that you cried unto me in your heart, that you might know concerning the truth of these things. Did I not speak peace to your mind concerning the matter? What greater witness can you have than from God?"[18]

Here is an example of this familiar means of personal revelation. Miriam was experiencing a great deal of emotional stress—she felt very ill at ease with the goings-on in her life. She had trepidation about the family's upcoming move to another state. Also, she was filled with concerns about her daughter serving a full-time mission.

---

17. Genesis 41:16.
18. D&C 6:22-23; See also D&C 19:23.

In an attempt to find some peace of mind, Miriam attended the temple. While in the temple, in answer to her prayers of concern, she "heard" a voice that said, "You will be fine. You really will be fine." Having received those specific words of peace to her mind, Miriam's burden of emotional stress was lifted, her heart was no longer troubled—and she was fine.

Peace is clarity of mind and heart—there is no confusion and there is no doubt. The principle is that peace of mind comes when it is needed most—when there is stress or turmoil or when there is pain or suffering. When someone is at peace, he or she experiences an emotional and mental confidence that all is right or will be right, even when events in his or her life appear to be going poorly. There are a couple of stories that can be used to illustrate this point. The first can be found in the Book of Mormon. The Nephites were at war with the Lamanites. Fortunately, Helaman, the son of Alma the younger, was the Nephite leader. Helaman records that, in the middle of the conflict, he and his fellow warriors poured out their souls to God in prayer, seeking strength and deliverance. In answer to their prayers, they received the assurances they sought as God spoke "peace to our souls. . . ." (Alma 58:11) Elder Rex D. Pinegar tells the second story of peace being found in the midst of adversity:

> It was a happy, carefree time in my young life until on such a day, sorrow and tragedy brought me closer to God in humble, sincere prayer. In the summer of my thirteenth year, on a July night, I eagerly joined some neighborhood friends to light fireworks. Five of us took turns igniting the colorful assortment of Roman candles and rockets and firecrackers. Each was a new surprise with its burst of sights and sounds through the evening sky.
>
> Not all of our fireworks worked as they should have. Most, in fact, were what we called duds. They sputtered momentarily, and then died. We set the duds aside until we had tried to light all of the fireworks. We had so many defective ones remaining, we wondered what to do. We couldn't just throw them away. What if we emptied the powder from all of them into the cardboard box? We could toss in a match and have one gigantic blast!
>
> Fortunately for us, our idea failed—at first. The match was tossed; we quickly ran away and waited. Nothing happened. Pressing our luck, we tried a second time, using a makeshift fuse

of rolled-up newspaper. Again we anxiously waited at a distance. Again, to our good, nothing happened. That is when we should have quit. Foolishly, we gave it one more try; this time my friend Mark and I huddled around the box to keep the flame from being extinguished by the evening breeze.

Then it happened! The "gigantic blast" we thought we wanted exploded with fury into our faces. The force of the explosion knocked us off our feet, and flames from the ignited powder burned us severely. It was a tragic scene. Responding quickly to the screams and cries of the injured youth in her driveway, our friend's mother gathered us into her home. "First we will pray," she said, "and then we will call the doctor."

That was the first of many prayers I remember being offered for us. Soon after, I felt my face, hands, and arms being wrapped in bandages. I heard the voices of my father and my doctor administering a priesthood blessing to me. I heard my mother's voice many times, pleading with Heavenly Father to please let her son see again.

I had been taught very early in my life to pray. Mother and Father had made prayer an important part of our family life. Not until that day, however, did it become so meaningful to me. In those frightening moments I found peace and comfort through prayer.[19]

Just as speaking peace to one's mind is a common means Heavenly Father uses to answer prayers, likewise, the absence of peace, or a feeling of unease, conflict or dread is also a means of revelation. When I was out of work for the second time, I remember struggling to locate a job that would provide for my family. After five months of diligent searching, I was offered a position with a large property management company. In some respects, this was a direct answer to

---

19. Rex D. Pinegar, General Conference Report, "Peace Through Prayer," *Ensign,* May 1993, 65. This story reminded Elder Pinegar of Alexandre Dumas, in his classic tale *The Count of Monte Cristo,* who wrote, "For the happy man prayer is only a jumble of words, until the day when sorrow comes to explain to him the sublime language by means of which he speaks to God." (Trans. Lowell Bair, New York: Bantam Books, 1981, 34)

my many prayers—a job offer. Unfortunately, the compensation offered by the company was insufficient to take care of my family's basic financial needs. Our financial needs were not great—in fact, our only indebtedness was a modest house payment. This circumstance made me sense that there might be some truth to the statement that any income is better than no income.

In this case, the opportunity for me to have at least some income was accompanied by nagging, oppressive feelings of unease. So absent was my peace of mind that I seemed to have no choice—there was no way I could accept the job offer. It was not until I turned down the offer that the weighty, dark and depressing feeling was lifted from me. Within three weeks, following a series of mini-miracles, I was extended a job offer from a company in a different industry, at a level of compensation that was adequate for our family's financial requirements. To this very day I can still feel the peace of mind that came by not accepting that particular job offer, as well as the tremendous joy and peace of mind that came from being gainfully employed.

Peace of mind is a powerful tool. President Thomas S. Monson has taught that prayer is the passport to such peace.[20] This frequent means of answering one's prayers is a means of revelation that the Savior intended for our benefit. He intentionally speaks peace to our minds so that our hearts will neither be troubled nor afraid.[21]

The Spirit Speaks with a Still Small Voice

Impressions and feelings may be communicated to and felt in one's heart. Also, peace may be spoken to one's mind. When an individual recognizes impressions on the heart as personal revelation or inspiration, such impressions are to be acted upon. When such impressions are acted upon, one is prepared to receive more detailed directions to the mind that will strengthen the impressions received in the heart. To do this the Lord may speak peace to a person's mind or provide other instruction.

---

20. Thomas S. Monson, General Conference Report, "The Path to Peace," *Ensign,* May 1994, 60.

21. John 14:27.

This is a very common and effective way Heavenly Father answers prayers in a discernable manner—he speaks to people. The apostle John recorded, "Behold, I stand at the door, and knock: if any man *hear my voice,* and open the door, I will come in to him, and will sup with him, and he with me." (Revelation 3:20, emphasis added) Unlike impressions to the heart, revelation to the mind comes to us in specifics, not generalities. Whether the revelation is an audible voice or not, when received by our minds, such communication will come as a discernable thought or impression in one or more whole sentences.[22] The following story is an excellent example of this point, as told by Grant E. Barton:

> I was fourteen and had tried to catch a bus to visit my father, who was stationed at an army base in Tooele, Utah, some thirty-five miles from Salt Lake City. I missed the bus, however, and decided to hitch a ride instead. A man took me as far as the Great Salt Lake and dropped me off near a smelter about twenty miles west of the city. It began to rain and night was descending. Sulfuric fumes from the smelter filled the air, and I began to cough and wheeze.
>
> Remembering my parents' teachings, I started to pray. As I struggled for breath, my prayers became more desperate and earnest.
>
> Into my mind came a voice that said, "Run." I didn't feel like running and shrugged off the impression. But the voice repeated more distinctly, "Run." I started to jog through the cold rain. The voice came again and said more urgently, "Run as fast as you can!" So I did.
>
> As I staggered over the top of a hill, I saw a lone car in the process of making a U-turn. I croaked out a noise and waved my arms. The car stopped, and even though I couldn't speak coherently, the kindly couple in the car seemed to understand, invited me in, and drove away from the fumes. I was thoroughly drenched and was shaking uncontrollably from the cold. The couple told me that they had been sitting in their home in Tooele

---

22. See Enos 1:5, 10. Elder Marion G. Romney said that when our understanding is enlightened by the power of the Spirit, "It comes into one's mind speaking words and sentences." (*Ensign,* Sep. 1999, 12)

and felt that they should take a drive—in the middle of the storm![23]

Many can probably recall instances that allow them to say, "Yes, that is exactly what happened to me, a voice came to me."[24] When they have such an experience, they may be uncertain whether they heard the words or whether the words came as silent thoughts in their minds. There may even be some discussion as to whether the voice was audible or not. Even if it were not audible, that kind of voice is still heard. The scriptures teach that this is so: "And it came to pass when they *heard* this voice, and beheld that it was not a voice of thunder, neither was it a voice of a great tumultuous noise, but behold, it was a still voice of perfect mildness, as if it had been a whisper, and it did pierce even to the very soul." (Helaman 5:30, emphasis added)

There is an excellent story about this still, small voice. Amber, as a young girl, worked on the family farm alongside her dad, brothers and sisters. She was given much responsibility at an early age, including the responsibility of operating some of the heavy machinery. This is how Amber tells the story:

> By the age of twelve I had moved up the ladder of responsibility to the position of "baler." My responsibility was to make sure that the windrows of cut hay were neatly made into round bales. Most of the time the equipment ran very well, however, there were times when my mechanical abilities were tested. It usually did not take me long to assess a situation and decide whether or not it was something that I could solve independent of the "real" mechanics.
>
> On this particular day, the tying mechanism of the baler malfunctioned. Instead of the end of the string catching between the large feeding rollers and wrapping nicely around the bale, it caught on one of the rollers and wrapped nicely around it. My efforts to free the string and properly bind the bale

---

23. Grant E. Barton, "On Bended Knee," *Ensign,* Feb. 1996, 50.

24. See Helaman 10:3. There may be a fine line between hearing an audible voice and a voice coming into our minds via specific thoughts and words.

were unsuccessful. As a result, I released the unbound bale and left the tailgate up so that I could have easy access to the string-covered roller. This left me in a precarious working position inside the bale compartment of the baler, directly under the tailgate.

Several minutes into the task, a thought came to my mind that I should work at removing the string from the other side of the baler. Without hesitation, I went to the front of the baler. Just as I was about to continue my efforts, the heavy tailgate slammed shut. Simultaneously, an enormous spray of hydraulic fluid shot through the air because a severely worn hydraulic hose had ruptured. The rupture caused the hydraulic system to fail. The weight of the tailgate could not be sustained, causing it to slam shut.

I reassessed the string situation and realized that I needed to go to the driver's cab to get a different cutting tool to free the bound string. As I climbed the steps to the cab of that John Deere, I realized what had just happened. I sat quietly in that well-worn seat, knowing that it was a miracle that I was still alive. Had I not immediately acted upon the crucial thought to change my position, I would surely have been crushed. Without any fear or worry about what could have happened, I knew that someone was with me, someone who was on my team. I know that through the spirit of the Holy Ghost, I was gently guided out of harm's way.

The voice that the Lord's people will hear will always be still and small—no screams, shouts or loud exclamations.[25] This voice may be so still and small as to be almost undetectable by our physical senses; nevertheless, it can be a very powerful communicator. When audible, it will never be harsh and will not be louder than a whisper. This is consistent with the way the Holy Ghost speaks to people—quietly, calmly, reverently and peacefully. However quiet and peaceful the voice may be, this means of revelation has great physical power. The still, small voice can whisper through and pierce all things, as well as make the body's bones quake.[26] This kind of voice

---

25. 1 Kings 19:11-12.
26. D&C 85:6.

is so powerful it can also pierce a person to their soul and cause their heart to burn.[27]

From my personal experiences, let me share the following story. It was a regular workday as I awoke and slowly rolled out of bed to a kneeling position at the side of my bed. I wanted to pray for the right thing and asked what I should accomplish at work that day. As clear as day, the specific words quietly came to my mind saying, "Handle the two Michigan annual reports." To my knowledge, I was not physically affected by the still small voice that came to my mind. At work that day, the first meaningful thing I accomplished was the paperwork delineated in the answer to my prayer received earlier that morning. There is no flashy ending to this little story. All I have to offer is my testimony that the Lord sometimes answers our prayers by way of a still small voice. The only specific blessing that I received from this ordinary experience is the peace of mind of having acted upon the direction given.

Why is this divine, noble voice so still and small? By being still and small, this quiet voice requires the hearer to pay closer attention to what may be said. This point is best illustrated when one recalls an effective public speaker or a skilled salesman. Such a person will at times intentionally lower his voice, almost to a whisper, in order to cause the listener to lean forward and make a greater effort to hear exactly what the person is trying to say. So it may be with the still, small voice; however, to reiterate, harsh, loud, or boisterous expressions are not, never have been, and never will be the Lord's way when using a voice to answer prayers.

Another reason the voice of the Spirit is so still and small is to teach us to seek out the whisperings of the Spirit. There is a story of a man sitting on a bench in a beautiful park on a lovely spring day. People are playing with their children, walking their dogs, riding their bikes and playing various games. The man on the bench is listening to the beautiful sounds of the birds in the trees—it is music to his ears, but no one else seems to hear those sounds. The man reaches into his pocket, pulls out a handful of coins and lets them drop to

27. 3 Nephi 11:3.

the sidewalk. Suddenly, people turn their heads in the direction of the sound of the money as it hits the concrete sidewalk and rolls along the ground.

The sweet sounds of the birds in the park went unnoticed by the people; however their attention was immediately captured by the sound of the coins striking the ground. So it is with the gentle voice of the Spirit and the various sounds of the world. In order that an individual may discern the closeness and content of the whisperings of the Spirit, that individual must attune him or herself to that still and small voice so that he or she is naturally inclined to recognize it above the distracting voices of the world.

Lastly, the still small voice is brief and concise. Rarely does one hear of experiences where the Spirit speaks in a lengthy series of sentences. Consequently, it will be unusual for the Spirit to say, "First, go to the East Side of town via Yale Avenue. Then go south on Cook Street. After going south three blocks, knock on the black front door of the house at 3058 South Cook Street." Although such experiences are possible, this is not usually the way the Lord will answer prayers. Most of the time, the specific direction to a person's mind will be modest in quantity—it will receive brief instruction through simple phrases.[28]

The Spirit Tells Us Simultaneously in Our Minds and in Our Hearts

Discernable answers to prayers may come as feelings in the heart, as peace of mind, or via that voice of perfect mildness, the still small voice. While such revelation may come by any one of these three methods, prayers may also be answered in another way. Personal revelation may come simultaneously to both the mind and the heart.

The concept of personal revelation simultaneously to the mind and heart is unique. Such a combination is often called the "voice of the Spirit" (1 Nephi 4:11-18). "The voice of the Spirit is a still, small voice—a voice that is felt rather than heard. It is a spiritual voice that

---

28. See 1 Ne 4:1-18.

comes into the mind as a thought put into your heart."[29] This voice is so unique that it is one of perfect mildness, as if it were a whisper, yet it can simultaneously pierce our very soul so as to reach our hearts.[30] It is this voice of the Spirit that allows us to "feel" the words that come into our minds. (1 Nephi 17:45)

In his instruction to Oliver Cowdery, the Lord revealed, "Yea, behold, I will tell you in your mind *and* in your heart, by the Holy Ghost, which shall come upon you and which shall dwell in your heart. Now, behold, this is the spirit of revelation." (D&C 8:2-3, emphasis added) It is a wonderful and reassuring experience when impressions come to the mind while at the same time the heart experiences a feeling consistent with one's thoughts. When the mind and the heart receive the same impression—when thoughts and understandings are congruent with feelings—one can know that he or she is receiving personal revelation. This is exactly what the Savior taught Hyrum Smith when he said, "I will impart unto you of my Spirit, which shall enlighten your mind, which shall fill your soul with joy" (D&C 11:13).

Elder Jay E. Jensen confirms this understanding of the scriptures when he says, "When the Holy Ghost speaks, our minds may be struck with insight and clarity akin to sudden light. At the same time, our hearts may burn or we may feel flooded with joy or deep gratitude or love. Whatever particular feelings occur, they occur simultaneously in the mind and in the heart."[31] When receiving such personal revelation, the words to the mind and the feelings in the heart will be consistent. There will be no conflict or inconsistency in the Lord's answer, when delivered to the heart and the mind simultaneously. Several examples of this type of discernable answer to prayers come to mind.

The first example is an experience of mine that took place at the end of a very long job search, and only a couple of weeks after I had

---

29. Boyd K. Packer, General Conference Report, "The Cloven Tongues of Fire," *Ensign,* May 2000, 8.

30. Helaman 5:30.

31. Jay E. Jensen, "Have I Received an Answer from the Spirit?" *Ensign,* Apr. 1989, 22.

turned down an earlier job offer. Little events led me to a job interview with a small, high-tech company. I prayed mightily leading up to that interview. When the day came, the interview was enormously successful. That very day I received the job offer, I knew in my mind that it was right, and was almost delirious with joy that I once again had a job. To this day, our family remembers the great celebration we had in our home that night as we dined on pizza delivered to our house.

I recall another example of this type of revelation. It was during a Saturday afternoon Priesthood Leadership meeting held in conjunction with our Stake Conference. A priesthood leader had attempted to teach us Church doctrine from the scriptures. During the course of the meeting, I "knew" in my mind that what I was being taught was not correct—that the scriptures were being improperly interpreted. In addition, I felt terrible inside about what was being taught. Something was definitely wrong. I felt sorry and embarrassed for the man doing the teaching. To complicate matters, this was a priesthood leader of responsibility who, by his office, deserved my respect. Consequently, I left that meeting feeling confused—filled with doubt about my own thoughts and feelings. After all, who was I to doubt or question such a priesthood leader? My confusion was cleared up some years later when I learned that this brother had lost his membership in the Church. Such news, although unexpected, did not come as a surprise to me. It made me reflect and realize from my experience years earlier that I can trust the simultaneous congruency between the thoughts of my mind and the feelings in my heart.

The third example is the story told by Jody, a young married woman who was anxious and ready to have her first baby. Following several miscarriages, Jody found herself pregnant again. She had been reading the scriptures and was prompted to pray, because she wanted to know what was to come of this pregnancy. This was a worrisome moment for Jody, because she knew that she had to trust whatever answer would come without being angry with God. As Jody talked to me about this experience, she made an interesting statement about this moment in her life. She recalled, "I knew my heart was right." In her prayer, all Jody asked was whether or not she would be having this baby? She was confident that Heavenly Father said, "No."

That night, Jody cried herself to sleep, not being angry with God, but mourning yet again the upcoming loss. Over time, she prepared for the pending miscarriage—a miscarriage that never came. For some time, she doubted the answer that she was confident she had received to her previous prayer. The answer in her mind and the emotion in her heart were consistent with one another—after all, sadness is not always a negative emotion, it is a very real sentiment accompanying a loss. Jody continued wondering, wondering if the trial would come by giving birth to a stillborn baby. More time passed. At long last, Jody gave birth to their first healthy baby.

This story can be understood in a couple of ways. Either the sadness that Jody felt in her heart simultaneously with the "no" answer she received in her mind cannot be categorized as a positive feeling such as understanding or peace, or, as her husband concluded, this may have been for her an Abrahamic test.[32]

The focus on this method of personal revelation is on the congruency between the thoughts in one's mind and the emotions or feelings in one's heart. This combination or congruency could accurately be called a feeling of understanding. The Lord teaches us this congruency as follows: "I will impart unto you of my Spirit which shall enlighten your mind, which shall fill your soul with joy; And then shall ye know, or by this shall you know, all things whatsoever you desire of me, which are pertaining unto things of righteousness, in faith believing in me that you shall receive." (D&C 11:12-14)

The personal experience that I had at stake conference is a confirmation of this very process of revelation. Since my mind was perplexed rather than clear on the doctrine being taught, and since my

---

32. "You will have all kinds of trials to pass through. And it is quite as necessary for you to be tried as it was for Abraham and other men of God. . . . God will feel after you and he will take hold of you and wrench your very heart strings, and if you cannot stand it you will not be fit for an inheritance in the Celestial Kingdom of God." (Joseph Smith as quoted by Larry E. Dahl, "The Abrahamic Test, " *A Witness of Jesus Christ,* Salt Lake City: Deseret Book Company, 1990, 53)

heart was filled with doubt and embarrassment rather than joy or peace, I could conclude that my mind was not being enlightened—that truth was not being revealed to me. I was being "revealed to" all right, but the message was, "You are not being taught true doctrine." On the other hand, the answer to my job-hunting prayer was a marvelous combination of "knowing" in my mind and feeling extreme joy in my heart—I was enlightened that this was the job for me.

The Spirit Occupies Our Minds and Presses upon Our Feelings

The Spirit does not make itself heard by shouts, screams or loud exclamations. Instead, as Elder Boyd K. Packer puts it, "It caresses so gently that if we are preoccupied we may not feel it at all. Occasionally it will press just firmly enough for us to pay heed. But most of the time, if we do not heed the gentle feeling, the Spirit will withdraw and wait until we come seeking and listening and say in our manner and expression, like Samuel of ancient times, 'Speak, Lord, for thy servant heareth.' (1 Sam. 3:10)"[33]

The gentle pressings of the Spirit generate a compelling feeling characterized by a sense of restlessness or perhaps a sense of urgency to do something specific. An excellent illustration of someone being influenced by the Spirit in this manner is Joseph Smith's reaction to reading James 1:5 in the Bible. Joseph's own words describe the motivating force of this passage of scripture: "Never did any passage of scripture come with more power to the heart of man than this did at this time to mine. It seemed to enter with great force into every feeling of my heart. I reflected on it again and again, knowing that if any person needed wisdom from God, I did; for how to act I did not know, and unless I could get more wisdom than I then had, I would never know." (Joseph Smith—History 1:12)

When the Spirit occupies our mind and presses upon our feelings, it serves as inspiration—a motivation to act in accordance with the specific promptings. As the Spirit acted upon Joseph Smith after reading the Bible, he was motivated to pray. In like manner, on

33. Boyd K. Packer, "The Candle of the Lord," *Ensign,* Jan. 1983, 53.

another occasion, he was motivated to implement certain administrative procedures regarding baptisms for the dead.[34]

Carol, a new Stake Primary President, who was trying to decide on her First Counselor, similarly felt the pressings of the Spirit. Even though her decision was the subject of extensive prayer, she seemed to be getting nowhere. While she was going through this process, the face of a beautiful woman with dark hair kept coming to her mind's eye. Carol gave no meaning to this face, although she tried to describe it to her husband to see if the face were familiar to him. It was not.

Meeting with the former primary president, Carol asked her about potential counselor candidates. The former president suggested a woman from her ward. Upon hearing the woman's name, Carol knew that that woman should be one of her counselors. Carol asked that she describe this sister to her. The former primary president described the same woman with the beautiful face and dark hair—the exact image Carol had been seeing in her mind.

Another way the Spirit occupies the mind is by enlightenment. This is accomplished whenever there is an increase in light, knowledge, and understanding on a particular matter. The Savior instructed Oliver Cowdery, "I did enlighten thy mind; and now I tell thee these things that thou mayest know that thou hast been enlightened by the Spirit of truth." (D&C 6:15)

Sometimes, this type of revelation comes when someone feels he is at his wit's end. In one's day-to-day life, circumstances beyond one's control may deter the person from putting adequate time and energy into a job, a class or a particular assignment. Church responsibilities, illness, family problems, or other unusual circumstances may create an additional need to call upon Heavenly Father for assistance. Steven D. Bennion, former president of Ricks College, recounts one such incident. He had been serving as a bishop, completing classes for his Ph.D., and working full-time to support his family of seven. He needed to finish his doctoral dissertation and defend it; unfortunately, the process was taking much more time than he had anticipated. Consequently, he had to apply an eleventh

34. D&C 128:1.

hour, full-court press to finish the effort. With only two days left, there seemed to be more work required than the allotted time available to complete it. Brother Bennion finishes the story this way:

> The first day was an exercise in frustration. I struggled at length through that day and produced only 4 pages. By 9 o'clock that evening, I was discouraged and desperate: I had only two nights and a day left to compose a compelling concluding chapter. I decided to get a good night's rest the first night, leaving myself only a day and a night to complete the chapter. I remember offering special prayers both that evening and the next morning. I pleaded my need to the Lord, reminding him of my good wife and family and their faithful support while I worked on the dissertation and served as bishop. I acknowledged gratitude for opportunities and then asked for special spiritual help to quicken my mind and spirit for the monumental challenge of completing the final chapter in a single day.
>
> I arose the next morning at 4:30 and began to write. The words flowed as I had never before experienced. The next 42 pages came far more easily than the first 4 had the day before.[35]

While Brother Bennion prayed and meditated upon his dissertation, the Lord touched the eyes of his understanding and they were opened, allowing him to complete his project within the available time constraints. The Prophet Joseph Smith observed that this is like pure intelligence flowing to a person. Said the prophet, "it may give you sudden strokes of ideas, so that by noticing it, you may find it fulfilled the same day or soon; (i.e) those things that were presented unto your minds by the Spirit of God, will come to pass; and thus by learning the Spirit of God and understanding it, you may grow into the principle of revelation, until you become perfect in Christ Jesus."[36]

---

35. Sally Taylor, *Speeches,* "The Holy Ghost: Our Infallible Guide," BYU Devotional Address, 5 Nov. 1996. (Steven D. Bennion, "Human Life Divided by Reason Leaves a Remainder," *Expressions of Faith: Testimonies of Latter-day Saint Scholars,* Salt Lake City: Deseret Book, 1996, 50)

36. *History of the Church* 3:381.

My personal experience in this area is limited—only one experience comes to mind. While serving as Bishop, I was in my makeshift office located in the basement of our home. It was early in the evening, after a full Sunday of regular meetings and interviews. I received the distinct impression to make a telephone call to a particular member of my ward to set up an appointment later in the week. The individual was home, allowing me to make the first of several appointments that we would have over the months that followed. At the time of the impression, I had no thought that I was having a spiritual experience, even though I do not recall any other time while serving as Bishop that I was impressed or prompted to telephone any other member of my ward. It was not until several weeks later that this member told me that on the day that I telephoned, the member had engaged in conduct that violated the moral code of the church. When that ward member answered my "out of the blue" telephone call that Sunday evening, that member knew that I was an inspired Bishop.

I was absolutely oblivious to the inspirational and spiritual ramifications of that singular impression and the accompanying phone call. It was a much more meaningful event for the church member involved. More importantly, it taught two things: first, the Spirit may occupy one's mind and press upon someone's feelings even when the person does not know it is happening; second, there is no requirement that the Spirit press upon one's feelings over an extended period of time. The important point is that the person acts, and that the person acts in accordance with the inspiration and promptings given.

The Spirit Constrains

To constrain means to either compel[37] or restrain.[38] When constrained, there are often unusual forces or pressures involved that cause someone to act or make specific choices.

When one is constrained by the Spirit not to do something, it is for our physical or spiritual safety that we are so restrained. Elder

37. Matt. 14:22.
38. Alma 14:11.

Dallin H. Oaks of the Quorum of the Twelve Apostles explains this principle: "We are often left to work out problems, without the dictation or specific direction of the Spirit. That is part of the experience we must have in mortality. Fortunately, we are never out of our Savior's sight, and if our judgment leads us to actions beyond the limits of what is permissible and if we are listening to the still small voice, the Lord will restrain us by the promptings of His Spirit."[39]

Elder Jensen tells a story about two missionaries that were one night walking along a familiar countryside road. "Suddenly, they both had an impression that they should go no farther in that direction. They retraced their steps and took another way home. The next day, they wondered why they had felt constrained to stop. They went back, this time in daylight, and found that, within a few feet of where they had stopped, a bridge had washed out."[40]

Being constrained and feeling constrained are two different matters. Feeling constrained can be an acknowledgement of the prompting, but without taking the necessary action as directed by the feeling. Being constrained, one takes the action one is compelled to take or stops doing what one is doing. What follows is Lisa's story about feeling constrained, but not being constrained.

Lisa was driving home on a narrow, two-lane road in north Michigan. It was 11:00 at night and very dark as she traveled along the tree-lined road. She felt constrained to stop, go back and get off that road immediately. The notion to stop and turn back did not make sense to her; consequently, she continued driving, disregarding the prompting she was given. Shortly thereafter, a car came at her from the opposite direction, driving directly toward her in her lane. Lisa was sure she was going to have a head-on collision. Somehow, she avoided a crash, but drove off the road, severely damaging her vehicle. Lisa was grateful to be unhurt, but regretted that she had not listened when she was clearly constrained by the Spirit.

When one is compelled to act, it can be difficult, because the prompted action may be unnatural or strained. For both the missionaries

---

39. Dallin H. Oaks, "Personal Revelation," *Ensign,* Sep. 1999, 10.

40. Jay E. Jensen, "Have I Received an Answer from the Spirit?" *Ensign,* Apr. 1989, 25.

and Lisa, it was a hassle and an inconvenience to follow the promptings of the Spirit. Following the Spirit can be very difficult to do when the prompting does not seem to make sense. People always seem to try to balance reason with the prompting—and that is the problem. Rather than trying to balance their personal, rational thoughts with the revelation, they will do better if they try to reason through the revelation.

Examining Lisa's experience, she may have said to herself, "I have received this prompting to get off this road; however, the road is clear, dry and safe, why should I not keep driving? Besides, if I turn back, I will get home thirty minutes later than I want to." This line of thinking rationalizes away the Lord's prompting.

If Lisa had focused solely on the prompting, she could have asked herself, "I have received this prompting—I wonder what it means? It must mean something important, otherwise I would not have received it. Could there be an obstruction or danger ahead? Is it important to follow such a prompting even if it does not make sense to me? Do I want to disregard the prompting just so that I can save thirty minutes of my time? Should I be immediately obedient to directives and guidance given by the Spirit?"

One time President N. Eldon Tanner felt constrained (compelled) to give a talk in General Conference on the Book of Mormon.[41] Even though he may have prepared a talk on another topic, it does not require much discussion to understand why he felt compelled to give such a talk.

On the other hand, when Nephi was constrained by the Spirit to kill Laban, the need to reason through the revelation was much greater. Nephi was directed three times by the Spirit to kill Laban. Nephi's first reason for not obeying immediately was that he, Nephi, had never killed anyone before. Nephi's second thought was, "Well, Laban did try to kill me, he refused to keep the commands of the Lord, and he took away all our family's property." The third stage of Nephi's reasoning allowed him to conclude that the Lord slays the

41. N. Eldon Tanner, General Conference Report, "Christ in America," *Ensign,* May 1975, 34.

wicked to bring about the Lord's righteousness. After reasoning through everything, Nephi realized that he "knew that the Lord had delivered Laban into my hands for this cause." (1 Nephi 4:17)

As with other revelations one may receive, the constraint will be clear even if it may not make sense. When the Spirit constrains someone, it is the person's responsibility to reason through the revelation, and obey the promptings of the Spirit.

The Spirit Causes Our Bosoms to Burn

The Spirit may also cause a physical burning or a feeling of compelling warmth in the chest or heart. Those attuned to the Spirit or sensitive to the Lord's presence may feel such a burning. Two of Jesus' disciples had such an experience when they were in his presence, even though they did not initially recognize him as the Savior. The disciples said to one another, "Did not our heart burn within us, while he talked with us by the way, and while he opened to us the scriptures?" (Luke 24:32)

In the Americas, Mormon described this warm, spiritual feeling experienced by those who recognized the still, small voice. He said, "It did pierce them to the very soul, and did cause their hearts to burn" (3 Nephi 11:3; See also Helaman 5:45). Such a feeling is a marvelous manifestation of the Spirit.

When one considers the burning in the bosom, Doctrine and Covenants 9:7-8 should be revisited. As one has learned, this method of revelation was specifically tailored for those engaged in the process of translation. When relied upon for non-translation purposes, the physical burning in one's heart or breast may or may not be experienced as an answer to one's prayer. Consequently, it may not be correct for us to apply these verses of scripture to the general process of receiving answers to our prayers. When the person who is seeking an answer to prayer improperly applies these verses, expecting or hoping for a burning feeling that does not come, frustration and disappointment may follow. Does the following story by Francine Bennion sound familiar?

> I met Bob when I was a sophomore at Brigham Young University. Without him, I found myself lonely in a crowd of my good friends; but with him, I recognized differences in our life-

styles that could promise a troubled marriage. Both of us wanted temple marriage, Church activity, a family, graduate education, time in the mountains, good music—we agreed upon the kinds of things in nice lists people construct to prove compatibility; but besides that, we shared curiosity and excitement about so many things that the world changed after we met. However, the differences were important enough to make our relationship considerably less than ideal.

When Bob asked me to marry him, I took his ring, then returned it, then took it back with misgivings. Not trusting my own decision, I asked God to confirm it for me. With all my soul I asked Him to give me a "burning feeling" in my heart if marrying Bob were right, or a "stupor of thought" if it were wrong; I experienced neither the burning feeling nor the stupor of thought. Wondering if my faith had been insufficient, I rephrased the question, asking if it was right to break off the engagement; again, I experienced neither burning nor stupor.

I prayed in my room; I prayed in the shower; I prayed high on a mountain I climbed alone; all my thought was "Please tell me if I have made the right decision. Please tell me what thou wouldst have me do." But I sensed not the slightest response.

Feeling abandoned, and not understanding why, I would have cried like David, had I known the words, "My God, my God, why hast thou forsaken me? why art thou so far from helping me, and from the words of my roaring? O my God, I cry in the daytime, but thou hearest not, and in the night season, and am not silent."

I didn't know the words at the time, but when I read them in the twenty-second Psalm years later I knew their meaning: if he had promised to answer my prayers, why had he forsaken me when I needed him most?

Twenty-one months after we had met, I married Bob in the Alberta Temple without receiving any recognizable assurance that doing so was right or that not doing so would be better. I made my own decision, committing myself to a relationship with risks and without any guarantees except the promises we made to each other before the most important witnesses. That commitment and those promises were mine, and I know now that I needed to make them without commandment to do so. I knew the Lord heard my prayer, so I didn't understand why he didn't tell

> me whether or not I should marry Bob. What I didn't understand was the difference between what I wanted and what I needed. I wanted to know if I should marry Bob. What I needed was a different lesson, and that's what the Lord was teaching me.
>
> I know now that I wanted God to take all the risk out of my marriage, and hoped that he would guarantee my good relationship with a husband. Instead, God required that I solve problems and make the commitment on my own. In the process of growing closer together, Bob and I have found adventure and sorrow, growth, identity, and a great joy. Most people need a positive answer that their choice of partner is right; I needed an answer of silence so I could grow in the ways I have mentioned. My situation is probably very rare. In most instances I'm certain it would be very unwise to move into an eternal marriage covenant without the sustaining testimony of the Holy Spirit.[42]

I do not want to weaken the potential impact this type of manifestation may have in the answering of our prayers. When I was in my early teens, I was one of a few youth in a small branch in Woodbridge, Virginia. I desperately wanted to know for myself that the church was the Lord's true church. Over a period of what seemed like several weeks, I lay in my bed at night and prayed before I went to sleep. I prayed that I could know, as Joseph Smith had known, that the church was true. I figured that if he could have a great spiritual experience, so could I.

Then it happened. One Sunday afternoon during Fast and Testimony Meeting, I experienced a literal burning in my chest—a burning that moved me to stand and bear my testimony for the very first time. The burning was so strong and my heartbeat so forceful that I was compelled to stand and through my 14-year-old tears testify that I knew the church to be true. I never felt as though this experience was any less meaningful than that which Joseph Smith experienced. That first real spiritual experience remains fresh in my memory to this day and was repeated five or six more times before my full-time mission. I experienced that burning in my heart a few times on my mission, but have experienced it only twice since then.

---

42. Francine Bennion, "Stone or Bread?" *Ensign,* Jan. 1976, 38.

Because the workings of the Spirit may be very different for different people, there may be other discernable physical sensations that one may feel when the Holy Ghost is bearing witness of a particular truth or answer to a prayer. Such other physical sensations may be just as effective at indicating a witness of the Holy Ghost for one person as the burning in the breast is for another.

The burning in one's bosom delineated in D&C 9:8 may be primarily designed as a means of aiding in the translation of scripture—but not exclusively. It may also serve as a barometer of the presence of the Lord, or it may attend the presence of the Spirit or the whispering of the still, small voice.

The Ministering of Angels

Since the time of Adam, angels have ministered unto men and women in accordance with the directives of the Lord.[43] To this day, angels have not "ceased to minister unto the children of men." (Moroni 7:29) Ministering angels "speak by the power of the Holy Ghost; wherefore, they speak the words of Christ." (2 Nephi 32:3) These messengers may minister to men and women in person[44] or in their dreams.[45] Like Amaleki, and in keeping with the purpose of this book, everyone is exhorted to believe in revelations and the ministering of angels.[46] One may never know how many times ministering angels have been present without making known their divine identity.

The genesis of this very book came from the thought in my mind about a possible heavenly messenger appearing at my bedroom door. It is correct that I had the thought; however, I have never believed that I received a personal visit by a ministering angel. Whenever we entertain the notion of a visit of such a messenger, we must be most cautious. As one of our living Apostles has said, "You can be given false spiritual messages. There are counterfeit spirits

43. Alma 32:23.
44. 1 Nephi 3:29; 11:14; Mosiah 3:2; Alma 8:14, 10:7.
45. 1 Nephi 8:2.
46. Omni 1:25.

just as there are counterfeit angels. Be careful lest you be deceived, for the devil may come disguised as an angel of light."[47]

My closest encounter with a ministering angel occurred in the spring of 1987. Sitting in the car, parked in the street in front of our house, my wife and I were having a very serious and emotional discussion regarding important matters affecting our relationship. I recall that I was still holding onto the car keys with my right hand. I was frustrated and angry as I said, "I don't understand why we are struggling like this." As I said it, I slammed the car keys down on the car seat next to my right leg, causing Joy to flinch. Of course, Joy had been praying about our situation, asking Heavenly Father why we were required to endure such trials. Through her tears, she shared with me, "Because you are going to be the next bishop of our ward." While I never would have admitted it out loud, I knew the moment she uttered those words that what she said was true.

In that experience, I believe my wife served as a ministering angel, revealing things to me that I had never supposed. The truth that she made known immediately enlightened my mind and changed many things in my life. This knowledge caused the Spirit to occupy my mind and press upon my feelings for the next six months—until I was called to serve as the next bishop of our ward.

There is another illustration of ministering angels as a source of discernable answers to prayers. A sister in our branch, a brand new member of the church in north Michigan, told us of her conversion. One day she prayed, saying, "God, you need to show me what you want me to do and you need to make it really obvious." The following day, the fulltime missionaries from our branch knocked on her door. The truth of the gospel was taught, faithfully received and its message obeyed. Within a year's time, this sister, her husband and two of their children were baptized. Did not these missionaries serve as ministering angels to this faithful, searching sister?

---

47. Boyd K. Packer, "The Candle of the Lord," *Ensign,* Jan. 1983, 55.

Dreams

Another very interesting way God may answer prayers is through dreams. Through this method a man or woman may hear the voice of the Lord,[48] messengers may visit[49] or images may come to one's mind or appear in dreams.[50] An individual may also receive an answer by experiencing feelings in the heart through a dream.[51] Also, dreams may even foretell future events.[52] Cheryl had one of these experiences first-hand.

Cheryl was the Relief Society President of our ward and was a very close friend of a sister named Jean. Jean's husband was diagnosed with a severe cancerous condition—one that would require surgery. As the day of the surgery drew near, Jean and her husband were told that the surgery could last between four and fourteen hours, depending on the severity of the cancer. The night before the surgery, Cheryl dreamed that as she walked into the family waiting room to be with Jean, Jean stood, smiled at her and said, "The surgery lasted only four hours and everything is going to be OK."

The next morning Cheryl mentioned her dream to one of the sisters in the ward, but was afraid to say anything to Jean. She did not want to prematurely get Jean's hopes up. As good friends often do, Cheryl went to the hospital to be with Jean during the course of the surgery. After waiting what seemed a very long time, the doctor came into the surgical waiting room and told Jean and the family and friends that the surgery had lasted about four hours and that everything should be fine.

Experiences of this nature are partial fulfillment of the Lord's prophecy that "I will pour out my spirit upon all flesh; and your sons and your daughters shall prophesy, your old men shall dream dreams, your young men shall see visions." (Joel 2:32)

---

48. Genesis 20:3; Ether 9:3.
49. Genesis 31:11; Matthew 1:20.
50. Genesis 31:10.
51. Daniel 2:1, 3; 4:5.
52. Genesis 37:5-7, 9; 40:5; 41:7; Matthew 2:12-13.

Although dreams are one of the wondrous ways Heavenly Father may communicate with his people, dreams are perhaps the most unusual method he uses. I say this because I am a significant dreamer. I dream almost every night, often having several dreams during one night. Because I know how bizarre, abstract and unusually creative the content of a dream can be, it seems a most unusual way for God to communicate with man. However, for those who rarely dream at night, a single dream may be a powerful and meaningful way for the Lord to communicate with that person.

Because I dream so much, I have often tried to suggest in my prayers that Heavenly Father consider answering my prayers through my dreams. If such prayers have ever been answered in my dreams, I am not aware of it. To my knowledge, I have not had a single dream that I recognize as a personal revelation. None of my many dreams have even conveyed the slightest hint of having any particular meaning. The only significance I see in my dreams is the presence of some distinct patterns identified by my wife as she reviewed many of my dreams that I had recorded in a dream journal.

Since each of us has an easier time recognizing answers to prayers through certain methods over others, I have concluded that dreams are not the way God has chosen to communicate with me. Nevertheless, according to the teachings of today's authorities, it is clear that "The Lord reveals His will through dreams and visions, visitations, through angels, through His own voice, and through the voice of His servants."[53] On the subject of dreams, here is a story about President Wilford Woodruff as told by President Spencer W. Kimball:

> President Woodruff was one of the great spiritual giants of this dispensation. The Lord gave him many dreams and visions; he baptized thousands of converts, as was explained to us today, and he performed many, many miracles. Few men have enjoyed more of the guidance of the Holy Spirit than did President Woodruff.

---

53. Boyd K. Packer, General Conference Report, "Personal Revelation: The Gift, the Test, and the Promise," *Ensign,* Nov. 1994, 59.

> "When I was a boy eleven years old," President Woodruff says, "I had a very interesting dream, part of which was fulfilled to the very letter. In this dream I saw a great gulf, a place where all the world had to enter at death, before doing which they had to drop their worldly goods. I saw an aged man with a beaver hat and a broadcloth suit. The man looked very sorrowful. I saw him come with something on his back, which he had to drop among the general pile before he could enter the gulf. I was then but a boy. A few years after this my father and mother removed to Farmington, and there I saw that man. I knew him the moment I saw him. His name was Chauncy Deming. In a few years afterwards he was taken sick and died. I attended his funeral," President Woodruff said. "He was what you may call a miser, worth hundreds of thousands of dollars. When the coffin was being lowered into the grave my dream came to me, and that night his son-in-law found one hundred thousand dollars in a cellar belonging to the old man. I name this merely to show that in this dream I had manifested to me certain things that were true. I think of all the inhabitants of the world having to leave their goods when they come to the grave.
>
> "After this scene had passed before me I was placed in a great temple. It was called the kingdom of God. The first man who came to me was Uncle Ozem Woodruff and his wife whom I helped into the temple.
>
> "In process of time, after embracing the gospel, and while on my first mission to Tennessee, I told Brother Patten of my dream, who told me that in a few years I would meet that man and baptize him. That was fulfilled to the very letter, for I afterwards baptized my uncle and his wife and some of the children; also my own father and stepmother and stepsister; and a Methodist priest or class leader—in fact, I baptized everybody in my father's house. I merely mention this to show that dreams sometimes do come to pass in life."[54]

For centuries, God has revealed his will to men and women through dreams. There are both scriptural and personal experiences that testify to this means of communication. Everyone should give

54. Spencer W. Kimball, "Preparing for Service in the Church," *Ensign,* May 1979, 47.

his or her dreams serious consideration, because one's prayers may be regularly answered in this manner.

The Vapor of Darkness

Another way that prayers may be answered is when one feels that he or she is in the midst of a vapor of darkness.[55] This type of answer is similar to experiencing a feeling in one's heart that was discussed earlier; however, this is a unique feeling—it is an all-encompassing, brooding omnipresence. It could be described as a feeling of great unease or even a temporary depressive feeling.

Whenever someone feels this way—whenever the vapor of darkness is present—that person can know with certainty that the action he or she hopes to take, or the decision he or she is contemplating, is headed down the wrong road. The vapor of darkness is a close cousin of the stupor of thought spoken of in Doctrine and Covenants Section 9:9. One must keep in mind that the stupor of thought is generally a part of the formal revelatory process associated with the work of translation. Similar to the stupor of thought, when enveloped by the vapor of darkness, one feels unmotivated, lethargic and blah. Perhaps the best way to describe this is to say the person will feel "down."

Do you remember the experience I described earlier when I felt I should not accept a particular job offer? As I prayed about that job opportunity, it was as if I were in the center of a mist of darkness—there was no peace—the job opportunity was not right. The vapor of darkness was too strong. After I made the telephone call and regretfully turned down the position, the weight on my shoulders was lightened and the vapor of darkness dissipated.

There is another experience I had with the vapor of darkness. We wanted to buy a vehicle to replace our 12-year-old station wagon. It was late November, and, after much diligent hunting, we found a vehicle that we felt was the right one for our family, and at a fair price. Purchasing a vehicle was going to be a meaningful financial commitment for us; consequently, we made the purchase of the vehicle the subject of our personal and family prayers. I was

55. 3 Nephi 8:20.

excited at the prospect of purchasing a "new" car. I expected this to be an upbeat, exciting experience. Unfortunately for my excitement, a discouraging fog seemed to encompass me, one from under which I could not escape. This feeling was so strong that I can still remember slouching back in one of our living room chairs, thinking about the car purchase, feeling that oppressive cloud that seemed almost tangible. As a result, I knew that we should not go forward with the purchase of that vehicle. Elder Scott of the Quorum of the Twelve described my feelings in this manner: "If, in trust, we begin something which is not right, He will let us know before we have gone too far. We sense that help by recognizing troubled or uneasy feelings."[56]

With the Christmas holidays consuming my thoughts, the thrill and thoughts of buying a car drifted to the back of my mind. After the New Year, Joy and I continued our vehicle shopping at the same dealership where we found the vehicle that at one time caused such excitement. "Coincidentally," the very vehicle that had captured my emotions was still on the lot, and now carried a price tag $1,000 less than five weeks earlier. A few days later, after more prayers on the subject, we returned to the dealership and purchased our "new," used car. The feeling of foreboding was nowhere to be felt, completely replaced by a feeling of family excitement.

This is what can be learned from these experiences. (1) The vapor of darkness can be recognized as a direct answer to prayers.[57] (2) Everyone has the strength to obey the prompting provided, even when such a prompting faces stiff competition from one's selfish desires and emotional inclinations. (3) There is a feeling of relief and energy when a person recognizes a discernable answer to their prayers and obeys the counsel given.

---

56. Richard G. Scott, General Conference Report, "Learning to Recognize Answers to Prayer," *Ensign,* Nov. 1989, 32.

57. 1 Nephi 19:11.

7
The Practical Application

What to Look for

Now is a good time to consider several sample questions or matters that one might want to address in prayer, together with possible answers that an individual might receive. It is important to examine the question we want to ask because the very question itself will generally dictate the type of answer to look for. For example, questions looking for a "Yes" or "No" answer will be answered differently than questions that are looking for an explanation or answers to "what" or "why" questions.

Six sample questions are listed below, together with the types of discernable answers that one may receive in response to such questions. One must note that these are only sample questions, together with types of answers that someone might want to look for. As the author of these materials, I am not trying to put myself in the place of Heavenly Father. I am only trying to provide a ready and simple way to consider how possible answers to prayers may be communicated. Considering how these sample questions may be answered may help someone to better understand what to look for in anticipation of an answer. As one reviews the various answers that are provided to the sample questions, one will recognize similarities in a particular method of communication. Lastly, as one reviews these sample answers, everyone must recognize that these possible answers are not exclusive—they often overlap and work in harmony one with another. When dealing with such delicate matters of the spirit, everyone must keep in mind that each person is different in his or her circumstances, character, temperament, humility, spirituality, and sensitivity to the Spirit in its manifestations. As the New Testament teaches, one cannot predict exactly how the answer will come: "The wind bloweth where it listeth, and thou hearest the sound thereof, but canst not tell whence it cometh, and whither it goeth." (John 3:8.)

Here are the sample questions:

1. A woman asks, "Should I marry Fred?"

Scriptures:

The scriptures are always a good place to start. The scriptures will not say, "Yes, you should marry Fred." The scriptures will lead you to other considerations that may provide an answer.

Leaders:

Conference talks, messages from the First Presidency and counsel from local leaders may provide a specific answer. Typically, a leader cannot give a woman an answer that she must receive for herself. The leader, however, may provide insight as to what else the woman needs to do to receive her answer.

Feelings of the heart:

If God's answer is "Yes," the woman will receive a positive feeling in her heart that this is the right decision. If the answer is "No," she will experience no identifiable positive feeling or she may receive an identifiable negative feeling.

The Spirit speaks peace to our mind:

The woman may "hear" the Spirit tell her in her mind, "Yes, you will be happy if you marry Fred." Maybe the words will be, "Do not worry, everything will be OK when you marry Fred." If there is no peace of mind, then the answer is "No," or the answer will be provided by another means.

The Spirit speaks with a still, small voice:

This answer will be very specific. The quiet voice will say, "Yes, you should marry Fred." Or, the Spirit will whisper, "No, this is not right for you." The words will generally be few, but clear.

The Spirit tells us simultaneously in our minds and hearts:

The Spirit will answer, "Yes," and her heart will be happy and at peace, or, the Spirit will tell her "No," and the woman's feelings will tell her that marrying Fred is not the right course for her to pursue. When the Spirit responds to her mind and heart, there will be no conflict. The "words" and feelings will be congruent.

The Spirit occupies our minds and presses upon our feelings:

The woman will have a persistent thought and a similar persistent feeling that she should either marry or not marry Fred. If there is a nagging conflict between her mind and her feelings, the answer would be "No," or she may understand that her answer is coming by another method.

The Spirit constrains:

She will feel compelled either to marry or not marry Fred.

The Spirit causes our bosoms to burn:

This will generally not be your answer; however, the woman may feel a burning as an indicator that she is interpreting a scripture, a feeling or the meaning of an event in its proper spiritual context, thereby perhaps confirming a "Yes" or "No" answer.

Ministering of angels:

A ministering angel will give the woman a specific answer or will give her specific guidance as to what to do to receive the discernable answer.

Dreams:

Her answer may come in a dream by receiving the voice of the Lord, a messenger, an image, a feeling in her heart or a view of the future.

Vapor of darkness:

The woman will experience this brooding omnipresence only if the answer is "No."

2. A man asks, "How can I cope with my current loss or pain?"

Scriptures:

The scriptures are always a good place to start. They talk of faith, hope, patience, endurance, longsuffering and deliverance.

Leaders:

Conference talks, messages from the First Presidency and counsel from local leaders may provide a specific answer. They may also provide insight as to what the man needs to do to receive an answer.

Feelings of the heart:

This alone will generally not be the means by which the man receives an answer to his "how" question. The man may feel love, joy peace, gentleness, goodness, faith, meekness, hope, confidence or temperance, notwithstanding his pain.

The Spirit speaks peace to our mind:

Without a full explanation in answer to his question, the man will have peace of mind about his circumstances. He will not be troubled or afraid.

The Spirit speaks with a still, small voice:

Words or sentences may come to the man, giving a specific explanation or direction. He may "hear" the words that will tell him what he needs to do to cope with his loss or pain. This voice will be calm, peaceful and reverent.

The Spirit tells us simultaneously in our minds and hearts:

The voice of the Spirit will come to the man's mind, joined by a congruent feeling in his heart. The mind may hear, "You must be prepared to endure such pain for many years," while simultaneously the man feels in his heart that he will have the physical or emotional strength to endure such pain.

The Spirit occupies our minds and presses upon our feelings:

The man may have persistent thoughts for a period of days that this will be a lengthy process. The man's heart may even feel heavy at the thought of having to endure such pain. Or, he may also feel relieved just knowing that this experience requires a long-term commitment to endure to the end.

The Spirit constrains:

The man will feel compelled to do something specific or be restrained from doing something he is inclined to do, resulting in increased strength or capacity to cope with his circumstances.

The Spirit causes our bosoms to burn:

This will not generally be his answer; however, he may feel a burning as an indicator that he is interpreting a scripture, a feeling or the meaning of an event in its proper spiritual context as it relates to his circumstance.

Ministering of angels:

A ministering angel will give the man specific counsel on how to cope with his loss or pain, or it will give him specific guidance as to what to do to receive a discernable answer.

Dreams:

The man's answer may come in a dream by receiving the voice of the Lord, a messenger, an image, a feeling in his heart or a view of the future.

Vapor of darkness:

The man will experience this vapor of darkness if he is taking action or plans on taking action that will not be what his Heavenly Father wants him to do.

3. A teenage girl asks, "What should I say to mom and dad?"

Scriptures:

The scriptures are always a good place to start. They will help enlighten her mind and give her insight as to what she could or should say.

Leaders:

Conference talks, messages from the First Presidency and counsel from local leaders may provide a specific answer. They may also provide insight as to what else the girl needs to do to receive an answer.

Feelings of the heart:

Feelings in the teenager's heart will not be an answer to such a question that asks for specific direction. However, a feeling of love, joy, peace, etc., may follow a plan of action that has come to her mind as she ponders her circumstances.

The Spirit speaks peace to our mind:

After the girl has developed an appropriate plan of action as to what to say to mom or dad, the Spirit will speak peace to her mind—she will feel comfortable with her plan of action.

The Spirit speaks with a still, small voice:

The Spirit will whisper to the teenage girl what she should say to her mom and dad. The guidance may be, "Apologize to your Mom and Dad tonight." The voice of the Spirit may simply advise, "Tell the truth."

The Spirit tells us simultaneously in our minds and hearts:

The voice of the Spirit will come to her mind, joined by a congruent feeling in her heart. The mind may hear, "Tell them about the car," while she simultaneously feels that "she should tell them what they need to know."

The Spirit occupies our minds and presses upon our feelings:

Consistent thoughts provided by the Spirit will repeatedly fill the teenager's mind, and her heart will have consistent feelings to act or not act accordingly. Such thoughts and feelings may be either positive or negative. She may not be able to escape these persistent thoughts until she takes the action she feels impressed to take.

The Spirit constrains:

The teenager will feel compelled to act or not act. There will be a sense of urgency to do as constrained. There will not be time to mull things over.

The Spirit causes our bosoms to burn:

This will generally not be the teenager's answer; however, she may feel a burning as an indicator that she is interpreting a scripture, a feeling or the meaning of an event in its proper spiritual context as it relates to her circumstance.

Ministering of angels:

A ministering angel will give the girl specific counsel on what to tell her mom and dad or will give her specific guidance as to what to do in order that she may know what she should tell them.

Dreams:

The girl's answer may come in a dream by receiving the voice of the Lord, a messenger, an image, a feeling in her heart or a view of the future.

Vapor of darkness:

The teenage girl will experience this vapor of darkness if she is taking action or plans on taking action that will not be the action God wants her to take. She may also feel this brooding omnipresence if she resists taking the specific action she knows she ought to take.

4. A teenage boy asks, "Is the Church true?"

Scriptures:

The scriptures are always a very good place to start. They will enlighten the boy's mind and give him specific insight as to the Savior and the truthfulness of the restored gospel.

Leaders:

Conference talks, messages from the First Presidency and counsel from local leaders will provide specific answers. They may also provide insight as to what else the boy needs to do to receive an answer.

Feelings of the heart:

The young man will receive a positive feeling in his heart that the church is true. He will have strong feelings of love, joy and happiness if he asks sincerely. There is no other answer one can receive.

The Spirit speaks peace to our minds:

The teenager may "hear" the Spirit tell him in his mind, "Yes, the church is true." He will have peace of mind when he receives this answer.

The Spirit speaks with a still, small voice:

This answer will be very specific. The quiet voice will say, "Yes, the church is true." The words will generally be few, but clear.

The Spirit tells us simultaneously in our minds and hearts:

The Spirit will tell the boy, "Yes," and his heart will be happy and at peace. When the Spirit responds to his mind and heart, the "words" and feelings will be congruent, even if there is severe opposition from family or friends.

The Spirit occupies our minds and presses upon our feelings:

The teenage boy will have a persistent thought and a comparable persistent feeling that the church is true. He will be inclined to act upon those thoughts and feelings.

The Spirit constrains:

If the boy is not a member of the church, he will feel compelled to be baptized. If he is already baptized, the boy will feel an immediate, deeper commitment to live in accordance with the teachings and commandments of the gospel.

The Spirit causes our bosoms to burn:

This very well could be the boy's answer. The teenager may feel a burning in his heart or chest as an indicator that he is interpreting a scripture, a feeling or the meaning of an event in its proper spiritual context as it relates to his circumstance.

Ministering of angels:

A ministering angel will give the boy a specific "yes" answer or will give him specific guidance as to what he should do to receive a discernable answer.

Dreams:

The teenager's answer may come in a dream by receiving the voice of the Lord, a messenger, an image, a feeling in his heart or a view of the future.

Vapor of darkness:

With regard to this question, it is not possible for this to be the answer to the boy's prayer.

5. A quorum president asks, "Whom should I recommend as my first counselor?"

Scriptures:

The scriptures are always a very good place to start. They will not provide the quorum president with the name of the person he should recommend. They may, however, enlighten the president's mind and inspire him as to what he could or should do to learn the specific answer.

Leaders:

Conference talks, messages from the First Presidency will provide general guidance, but will not provide a specific answer. On the other hand, counsel from your local leaders may provide specific insight or answers. Leaders may also provide the president with insight as to what else he needs to do to receive an answer.

Feelings of the heart:

Feelings in his heart will not be an answer to "who" the president should recommend. Such feelings will only confirm (if positive) or disapprove (if negative) the name of an individual the president has in mind.

The Spirit speaks peace to our minds:

The quorum president will experience peace of mind only after he has come to a conclusion as to which person he should recommend. If it is the right person, his mind will be at peace, not troubled or confused.

The Spirit speaks with a still, small voice:

A specific name may be "spoken" to the quorum leader's mind. Also, if he is thinking of the wrong person, the Spirit may whisper to him, "That is not the right person." The specific answer will come in a calm, peaceful and reverent manner.

The Spirit tells us simultaneously in our minds and hearts:

The voice of the Spirit will come to the president's mind, joined by a congruent feeling in his heart. If the person's name that comes to his mind is the right name, it will be accompanied by a positive feeling in the quorum leader's heart. If the name is accompanied by a feeling of confusion or uncertainty, the name is not the correct name at this time.

The Spirit occupies our minds and presses upon our feelings:

The name of an individual will keep coming to the president's mind, nagging at him with an unyielding persistence.

The Spirit constrains:

The president may feel compelled to recommend a particular individual. Or, he may also feel very good about a particular individual, yet for some reason, something holds him back from recommending that particular person.

The Spirit causes our bosoms to burn:

This will generally not be your answer; however, he may feel a burning as an indicator that he is interpreting a scripture, a feeling or the meaning of an event in its proper spiritual context as it relates to this circumstance.

Ministering of angels:

A ministering angel may give you a specific answer by providing a person's name. If not, the president will be given specific guidance as to what to do to receive a discernable answer.

Dreams:

The answer may come to the quorum president in a dream by receiving the voice of the Lord, a messenger, an image, a feeling in his heart or a view of the future.

Vapor of darkness:

When the president has the right name in mind, the vapor of darkness will not be present. The vapor of darkness will be associated only with the names of the wrong persons to be recommended.

6. A mother asks, "Why am I experiencing this stress or hardship?"

Scriptures:

The scriptures are always a good place to start. They talk of faith, hope, patience, endurance, longsuffering and deliverance.

Leaders:

Conference talks, messages from the First Presidency and counsel from local leaders may provide a specific answer. They may also provide insight as to what the mother needs to do to receive an answer.

Feelings of the heart:

Feelings in the mother's heart will not be an answer to a "why" question such as this. Such feelings will only confirm answers that will come to her by other means.

The Spirit speaks peace to our minds:

The Spirit will speak peace to her mind only to confirm a proper answer that comes to the mother's mind or comes to her by some other means.

The Spirit speaks with a still, small voice:

The Spirit may provide a specific answer to such a question. The answer will be a calm, peaceful and reverent one.

The Spirit tells us simultaneously in our minds and hearts:

The voice of the Spirit will come to the mother's mind, joined by a congruent feeling in her heart. The feeling she receives in her heart may not be the one she wants to feel; however, it will be one that ratifies the specific answer given to her mind. Although the mother may not be pleased with the answer, her heart and mind will be as one.

The Spirit occupies our minds and presses upon our feelings:

A specific answer will constantly come to the mother's mind and a similar feeling will persist in her heart.

The Spirit constrains:

An answer to a "why" question will not come via constraint. She may, however, be constrained to do or not do something that will lead her to an answer.

The Spirit causes our bosoms to burn:

This will generally not be the mother's answer; however, she may feel a burning as an indicator that she is interpreting a scripture, a feeling or the meaning of an event in its proper spiritual context as it relates to her circumstances.

Ministering of angels:

A ministering angel may give her a specific answer. If not, she will be given specific guidance as to what to do to receive a discernable answer.

Dreams:

The mother's answer may come in a dream by receiving the voice of the Lord, a messenger, an image, a feeling in her heart or a view of the future.

Vapor of darkness:

This will generally not be the means by which the mother's answer comes. The vapor of darkness will be associated only with an answer that comes to her that is not the correct answer.

As one considers the many questions that he or she would like to ask, it is a good idea to write down such questions. One-by-one, the questions can be compared to the different ways these questions may be answered. By doing this, one will discover that there are certain types of answers that will not be the means by which the prayer will be answered. That is good. That will help a person avoid looking for or anticipating answers that will not come. This will allow the person to focus on those means by which the discernable answer will tend to be provided.

Considering all that has been presented in this chapter, always keep in mind that man's ways are not the Lord's ways. It is not the intent of these materials to attempt to limit the Lord's methods of answering someone's prayers by a mere list in a book. Heavenly Father has many ways and means at his disposal to answer every prayer. Used properly, this chapter will serve as a resource to everyone in his or her efforts to receive answers to prayers.

Notwithstanding the various means of communication that Heavenly Father may employ, the proclamation remains the same—there is an answer to every sincere prayer. As confirmed in the scriptures, everyone that asks receives an answer: "Verily, verily, I say unto thee, blessed art thou for what thou hast done; for thou has inquired of me, and behold as often as thou has inquired thou hast received instruction of my Spirit." (D&C 6:14.)

8
Patience and Action

Why Me? Strength and Deliverance

Many have suffered through trials in life that they never thought they would experience. Some may have lost a loved one well before they thought it was time for them to go. Others, as a spouse or child, have had to endure the break-up of a family by divorce. An accident or surgery may have caused great pain and suffering. Some may have endured a life-long illness that restricted their physical or mental capacities. Almost without exception, these experiences cause people to ask themselves or God in prayer, "Why?" "Why me, why this trial, why now?" Such individuals may even have become judgmental and asked, "Why not Fred, he doesn't live the Word of Wisdom, he doesn't keep the Sabbath Day holy, he doesn't work hard for his money, he doesn't pay a full tithing?" Some, who feel at times they are the victims in life, may ask, "What did I ever do to deserve this?"

It is not the purpose of this book to answer these questions. However, one of the purposes of this book is to help people learn how, through their own prayers, they can receive discernable answers to such questions. My life has allowed me to experience several job losses, two major shoulder surgeries, chronic arthritis, financial ups and downs, the unexpected death of a parent, stressful interpersonal relationships and watching my children deal with their personal and family struggles. I feel especially blessed, because the "why" questions do not trouble me. I recognize such events in my life as just that—events that have occurred with which I must cope. My main focus has been to learn what I can do to change my circumstances, ease the pain, or dissipate the stress. Yet, this effort alone has at times seemed impossible, as the burdens of life have pressed heavily on my emotions as well as my shoulders.

What is it that one can do to cope with the various battles and burdens of life? One of the better ways to handle such trials is to follow the pattern set by the Nephites when they faced their various enemies and challenges. The battles of the Nephites were much like life's trials. A prime example comes from the Nephites' dealings with the Gadianton robbers.[1] As soon as the Gadianton enemy (the Nephite trial or challenge) appeared to the Nephites, they knelt down and prayed to God that they would be spared and delivered from this enemy. The Nephites prayed early, not waiting till the eleventh hour to seek God's help. The Gadianton army believed the Nephites were afraid of them and had bowed down out of fear, but in this the enemy was gravely mistaken.

Because the Nephites had faith in and feared only their God, the Nephites did not fear the enemy. As a consequence, when their enemies rushed upon them, the Nephites were prepared, "and in the strength of the Lord," (3 Nephi 4:10) they met their challenge. The battle was fierce and the slaughter was great. Even though the Nephites did not escape injury or loss of life, they prevailed.

Obviously, a key element in the process of deliverance from trials is prayer—a prayer for strength and deliverance. One must recognize that the trial usually continues while one simultaneously strives to overcome fear and exercises greater faith. As the battle rages, the Lord will speak peace to one's soul giving courage to the individual that carries the hope of deliverance in his or her heart. The prophet Helaman explains how the Nephites handled these difficult circumstances:

> Therefore we did pour out our souls in prayer to God, that he would strengthen us and deliver us out of the hands of our enemies, yea, and also give us strength that we might retain our cities, and our lands, and our possessions, for the support of our people. Yea, and it came to pass that the Lord our God did visit us with assurances that he would deliver us; yea, insomuch that he did speak peace to our souls, and did grant unto us great faith, and did cause us that we should hope for our deliverance in him. (Alma 58:10-11)

---

1. 3 Nephi 4:8-14.

Several things can be learned from the Nephites. First, prayer is an essential element in the process of being delivered from trials.[2] Second, success at overcoming trials should be sought in accordance with God's will and strategy, not one's own.[3] Third, there are many different ways a person can be delivered.

One way a person can be delivered from a particular tribulation is that the Lord lightens one's burdens. He does this by strengthening the person, thereby increasing the individual's capacity to handle the hardship. The Lord can make the burden light by removing the burden or by making the person stronger so that the burden in fact feels lighter. Sometimes the burden is literally lightened; however, most of the time, it is the person that will be strengthened. After all, there is greater growth in strengthening the person than there is in reducing the weight of the burden on the person. Depending on what one needs and what the Lord's will is for a person, the person may be strengthened physically, mentally, academically, emotionally or spiritually as the circumstances require.[4]

Some may have an experience similar to Job's or to Alma's and Amulek's. Others may even be tried, as was Abraham. No matter what the trial, every faithful, repentant, prayerful person will ultimately be delivered. While the Lord's people are in the process of enduring, their burdens will somehow be made light, until they are delivered. The deliverance such people seek may not be obtained until they pass from this mortal life, but they will be delivered.

Wait and Listen for the Answer

A fine young man who had been home from his mission only a couple of years was in the middle of a sincere romantic relationship. On one occasion, he shared with me in a letter some frank feelings about the situation in his life: "My heart is dying. I'm dying. I can't even eat and I can barely drink. Sleep is at times out of the question. I have poured my heart out to God, and it seems that I'm receiving

2. See also 3 Nephi 3:15.
3. 3 Nephi 3:19-21.
4. Mosiah 24:10-15.

a busy signal from him. It is as if he is saying it's up to me to make things work. I am dumbfounded—completely dumbfounded and I have received little help. What shall I do?"

Among other comments, I advised him to be patient, wait and listen. This was hard advice to accept, especially when dealing with such delicate matters of the heart. The young man was patient, eventually receiving an answer to his many prayers. I do not recall how the answer came, but I do know that the romantic relationship developed into a marriage sealed in the St. George temple.

According to Elder Richard G. Scott, the answers to prayers will generally not come while one is still on his knees praying.[5] This can be difficult to accept because the matter about which a person is praying may, in that individual's judgment, require immediate action. Yet, the person is required to be patient. Often, instantaneous answers are sought through prayer. Elder Boyd K. Packer teaches us that such communication "can *never* be forced! If we try to force it, we may be deceived."[6] He also teaches that, "It is not wise to wrestle with the revelations with such insistence as to demand immediate answers or blessings to your liking. You cannot force spiritual things. Such words as compel, coerce, constrain, pressure, demand, do not describe our privileges with the Spirit. You can no more force the Spirit to respond than you can force a bean to sprout, or an egg to hatch before it's time. You can create a climate to foster growth, nourish, and protect; but you cannot force or compel: you must await the growth."[7]

There are times when the waiting will seem unbearable. There are times, when due to the particulars of a situation, the waiting will even be frightening. Nevertheless, one must wait and one must listen—remaining open to the promptings that will come. Unfortunately, many are not comfortable enough with the amount of

---

5. Richard G. Scott, General Conference Report, "The Power of a Strong Testimony," *Ensign,* Nov. 2001, 88.

6. Boyd K. Packer, General Conference Report, "Reverence Invites Revelation," *Ensign,* Nov. 1991, 21.

7. Boyd K. Packer, "The Candle of the Lord," *Ensign,* Jan. 1983, 53.

quietude and patience that is often required. In today's get-up-and-go lifestyles, quiet moments and periods of inactivity are often deemed to be wasteful. As an example, most people have heard someone stand up in a fast and testimony meeting and say, "I hate to see this time go to waste." As we grow in our spiritual sensitivity, perhaps one day we may hear someone stand and say, "Please excuse me for interrupting the silence and treading on this reverent moment."

Considering the need for both quietude and listening as essential elements in receiving answers to prayers, the Lord's admonition on the matter is humbling: "Be still and know that I am God." (D&C 101:16; 123:17) One more part of the waiting process may be Heavenly Father's desire to answer a prayer little by little, precept upon precept as he tries and proves the person, until he or she is ready for the full answer.[8]

An additional ingredient of the waiting experience is the need to keep moving and doing. This is important because there is a tendency for people to stop taking action while they are waiting for further direction. John H. Groberg explained this when he said, "We pray for good things and they don't seem to happen, so we sit and wait and do no more. We should always pray for help, but we should always listen for inspiration and impressions to proceed in ways different from those we may have thought of. We should never stop moving because we think our way is barred or the only door we can go through is closed."[9]

While waiting, one should keep moving in the direction the person feels inclined to go. If it is the wrong direction, the individual will be constrained or impressed to correct the course. Each person should do whatever can be done to help the Lord accomplish his purposes. While one does not have the duty to exhaust absolutely every known resource prior to receiving a revelation regarding a problem, one does have the responsibility to make a diligent effort to be an active part of the solution.

---

8. 2 Nephi 28:30; D&C 98:12; 93:13.
9. John H. Groberg, "The Lord's Wind," *Ensign,* Nov. 1993, 28.

My wife kept moving as she waited for an answer to her prayer. I was informed that after several more weeks, I would no longer have a job with my company. I was living in Salt Lake City at the time and my chances of finding suitable employment in my industry, in Salt Lake City, were meager at best. I was invited to interview with a small oil and gas company in northern Michigan. Following my interviewing trip to Michigan, I knew I would be offered a job and that I would accept the offer. After receiving the job offer, I told Joy that I was prepared to accept the offer. When she asked if I were going to fast about it, I said "No," because it was my feeling that the job offer itself was a direct answer to my prayer.

For Joy, it was different. Waiting for her own answer was important, because she needed to fast to receive a personal confirmation that the move to Michigan was the right decision for our family. At some point during her fast, the words of the hymn, "On this Day of Joy and Gladness," came to her mind. Joy, an accomplished pianist, went to the piano in our living room and began to play the hymn from the hymnbook. As she played the hymn she began to cry—because the message of the hymn was not the answer she wanted. Joy felt that the direct answer to her was that she should be glad at the opportunity for me to have continued employment and glad for the opportunity to move to Michigan. She had her answer, but she did not feel glad. Nevertheless, she willingly moved to Michigan, trusting in the Lord's answer to her prayer.

There are blessings that come to a person who waits. One such blessing is that the person defines himself as one of the Lord's people.[10] Another is that God strengthens one's heart in preparation for the feeling or impression it is about to receive.[11] Such a blessing is important if the Lord is considering asking the individual to do something that is powerfully against the person's own will. Such was the blessing my wife received in contemplation of the answer she would receive about moving to Michigan.

---

10. 2 Nephi 6:13.
11. Psalms 27:14.

An analogy can be drawn between the need to wait upon the Lord and the means by which information is transmitted across the Internet. Data passing through the Internet is divided into small packets of information that are sent across this vast web one packet at a time. For example, if someone were to send you this book across the Internet, the entire book would not be sent as a single lump of data. It would be broken down into packets—like sentences or clusters of words—that would be sent in random order from one computer to another. This process happens so fast, that one neither sees the book divided into its packets, nor the packets reassembled into an orderly written book by the receiving computer.

As a man or woman waits for answers to a prayer, he or she needs to be patient, listening to the small packets of promptings and spiritual data that will come. Only after the spiritual packets have arrived, line upon line, can the person discern the complete message Heavenly Father wants the person to receive. Part of the answer may come from the scriptures, part from church leaders, and another part from one's personal thought processes. When taken together, these packets of spiritual data or revelation will form a complete answer.

While an individual is waiting for an answer, is it not possible that it is actually God who is waiting on the individual? Could Heavenly Father be waiting on a man to develop a needed character trait? Could he be waiting on a woman to prepare her prayer better? Is he waiting on the home teacher to pray sincerely that God's will be done? Is he waiting on the Primary worker to push aside some of life's noises so that in quietude she can hear the answer? Is it possible that the person who is feeling impatient is the root cause of the waiting?

It may be a part of the nature of the natural man and woman to be impatient. Such impatience vis-à-vis the Lord is only exceeded by the Lord's patience with his children. As Heavenly Father waits for us, he does not give up trying to convey the discernable revelation that his children seek. This point is illustrated in the Book of Mormon, when the people of Nephi were gathered at the temple. As the people conversed with one another about the Savior, some of them heard a voice from heaven, but they did not understand it.

A second time, they heard a voice and, once again, they did not understand it. According to the scriptural account, it was not until after the third time of hearing the Lord's voice, that they understood it. Then, "As they understood they cast their eyes up again towards heaven." (3 Ne. 11:8)

The people of Nephi were most likely worthy, righteous people, who were at the temple, or on the temple grounds, during this event. Some of the people may have heard the voice before others, but only as they heard and as they understood did they look toward heaven and see the Savior descending. Heavenly Father understands our natures, repeats his directives as necessary and is many, many times more patient with us than we ever will be required to be with him.

A pleasant way to summarize the concept of patience following prayer is by reading the words of a poem by Eliza M. Hickok, titled "Prayer."[12]

> I know not by what methods rare
> But this I know, God answers prayer.
> I know that He has given His word,
> Which tells me prayer is always heard,
> And will be answered, soon or late.
> And so I pray and calmly wait.
> I know not if the blessing sought
> Will come in just the way I thought;
> But leave my prayers with Him alone,
> Whose will is wiser than my own,
> Assured that He will grant my quest,
> Or send some answer far more blessed.

My Ways Are Not Your Ways

The Prophet Joseph Smith taught, "Whatever God requires is right, no matter what it is, although we may not see the reason thereof till long after the events transpire."[13] The following story by

---

12. Eliza M. Hickok, "Prayer," *Ensign,* Feb. 1990, 5.

13. *Encyclopedia of Joseph Smith's Teachings,* Edited by Larry E. Dahl and Donald Q. Cannon, Salt Lake City: Bookcraft, Inc., 1997, 236.

Thomas Partridge provides an excellent example of the prophet's teaching:

> The term papers I needed to grade were nowhere to be found at home, and I knew I would not be able to rest until I located them. I had no inkling then of the lesson they would help me learn.
>
> My wife was just leaving to take our daughter to sing in a Christmas concert, and I realized that if I went too, I could go by my office to see if I had left the papers there. So I drove my wife, daughter, and three other choir members to the concert hall 20 miles away. Dropping them off, I swung by my office to search for the papers. I found nothing; they were not there either. Before leaving to rejoin my wife at the concert, I said a quick prayer that I would be able to find the papers when I returned home—though I had no idea where else to look—and that all would be well that evening.
>
> On the way home after the concert, it seemed we were alone on the freeway in the dark, snowy night. We had gone about a third of the way when the right front tire on our van blew out. Fortunately, I was able to control the vehicle and stop safely at the side of the road in the slush. It was 10:30 P.M.
>
> Opening the door, I said another silent prayer that all would be well and we could get home quickly. But it was not to be that easy. After working under the van for 45 minutes, I found that our jack would not fit in place with the tire fully deflated. As I worked, I made a silent observation to heaven that help would be welcome. A bit of bitterness swept over me when I finally realized that I was going to have to walk for help, soaking wet, through the night's cold to a service station a mile and a half away. Surely someone in one of the vehicles that passed us might have been prompted to stop—but it didn't happen.
>
> I walked to the station and called a tow truck. On my way back to the van, a highway patrolman picked me up and gave me a ride, and after the truck came and the tire was changed, I felt grateful at least that the tow truck driver had charged me a fair price for his help.
>
> By 12:30, my wife and daughter and I were at home getting warm, and I began to look once more for the lost term papers.

I felt prompted to look under a stack I had checked before. There they were!

Why, I wondered, had I gone through this experience? It would have been so much less stressful, so much more efficient if I had found the papers when I looked earlier.

Then suddenly in my mind's eye I saw my wife walking alone in a dress and heels down a dark, snowy freeway at 11:00 at night, having left four children alone in the van. Tears filled my eyes as I realized that perhaps Heavenly Father hadn't immediately given me what I had asked for, but rather what I would have wanted in my heart. I would have wanted to be there for my wife in that situation.

I had prayed for relief from immediate difficulties. Instead, I got what I really needed: the peace and assurance that comes from knowing that Heavenly Father is aware of and watching out for my family and me.[14]

When it comes to answering prayers, the Lord's ways are not man's ways; yet, how often does a person persist in his frustration and impatience simply because he will not acknowledge this truth and yield himself to God's ways? Only good can come from doing things the Lord's way. Heavenly Father will always guide us to do good, to do justly, to walk humbly and to judge righteously.[15] Whatever his counsel, it will always have a positive, favorable impact on people's lives and will always be in harmony with accepted revelations of the Church. This means that one should not be disappointed when a prayer is not answered the way one would like. That is because The Lord is always dealing with us in terms of our needs, not our wants. Here is an example from a story told by Stephen and Sandra Covey:

This is pretty hard doctrine for any of us, and it was especially hard for our teenage daughter. Being elected cheerleader of her high school seemed to be the most important need in her life. She had worked for several months, practicing every day

---

14. Thomas Partridge, "The Unexpected Answer," *Ensign,* Feb. 2002, 37.

15. D&C 11:12.

doing cartwheels, flips, splits, and cheers, till we were all relieved when the final cuts came. There were tears every time one of her close friends was eliminated and hope surged as she progressed to the final election assembly. "Oh, Mother, I'm praying so hard to win. The Lord says you can ask for any righteous desire of your heart and this is mine." It seemed a reasonable request to us, too. She was firm and solid in the Church and socially popular in a very sophisticated and large high school. We thought she would be a good influence for the Church.

At the final assembly tryout things went beautifully. She was in great form, her cheer was original, she was well known and received as much or more applause than anyone else. She seemed a cinch to be one of the five winners. She was absolutely crushed when she lost. It was only by a few votes, but she lost.

"Mother, you just don't know how important this was to me," she sobbed. "It's one of my lifetime goals. Why did the Lord let me down when I prayed so fervently? It wasn't just for myself. I was going to use this office as a good, solid influence for the Church. I study the scriptures every single night. I do missionary work constantly. I stand up for the Church in every situation; I work my head off in the ward and on the stake youth council and then one time I ask for help—what do I get? It isn't as if I didn't do my part. I practiced for six months. I couldn't have tried harder."

Sandra remembers, "I was a little disillusioned myself. So good. So faithful. So deserving. I didn't have too many answers, but I told her there must be a good reason and through prayer and study she would come to understand why."

The very next month she was asked to be one of the high school seminary officers. All of the seminary council had made personal sacrifices to serve. The seminary president had been asked to give up running for student body president; this was a hard decision for him. They said they really needed our daughter's creativity and missionary talents to draw people, and this year was a crucial one for gaining a positive stronghold.

That year she had many profound spiritual experiences. She developed deep, meaningful friendships and was a positive influence in helping several people come into Church activity.

> Later she told me that she gradually came to an understanding of herself through fervent prayer and study of the scriptures. "I wanted to be cheerleader more than anything else, but the Lord knew I needed this other experience more. I needed more spiritual growth. It was a hard experience, but I know in my heart it was right."[16]

It is imperative that people develop the teachable attitude that God's ways are different from their ways. There is a superb example of this principle in the scriptures. This example comes from the Lord's commandment to the Prophet Nephi to build a ship.[17] Nephi, having never before built a ship, was instructed to build a ship in the manner that would be shown to him by the Lord. As Nephi began to build the ship, his brothers, non-believers of the world, neither believed Nephi could do it, nor would they help him in the physical construction of the vessel.

Nephi's indolent brothers derided him, denied the Lord instructed him, claimed he was a fool, claimed he was incompetent for the task and determined him to be a man lacking in good judgment. Most people can imagine how Nephi felt because they have seen men or women struggle in the workplace when a manager intimated that a worker's idea was ridiculous or that the worker was incompetent or had exercised poor judgment. A good worker subjected to such treatment suffers a heavy emotional toll. Yet, this was the very kind of stress under which Nephi was working.

Like Joseph Smith, Nephi knew the truth and was able to withstand and work through the accompanying ridicule, feeling all the while that "If God had commanded me to do all things I could do them." (1 Ne. 17:50) What faith! Yet, compared to the many miracles God had performed, instructing Nephi how to build a ship was a simple task.[18]

---

16. Stephen R. and Sandra Covey, "Teaching Our Children to Pray," *Ensign,* Jan. 1976, 59.
17. 1 Nephi 17.
18. 1 Nephi 17:51.

Nephi built the ship, not as an experienced ship builder would build it, but as instructed by the Lord, praying regularly during the building process. The significance of this story comes after Nephi was finished building the ship. The completed vessel—built after the manner of the Lord, "was good, and the workmanship thereof was exceedingly fine." (1 Ne. 18:4) When we have faith, are obedient in following the discernable instructions given, we, as ordinary men and women, are capable of producing extraordinary results.

Even though God's ways are not man's ways, there is much confidence to be gained by performing pursuant to Heavenly Father's directions. Elder Boyd K. Packer teaches that "If we follow the promptings of the Spirit, we will be safe, whatever the future holds."[19] Whatever inspiration or revelation comes in answer to our prayers, an individual should not be alarmed because it was not what the person expected, even if the answer seems bizarre or embarrassing. If a woman asks for bread, God will not give her a stone. He may give her a bagel or ask the woman to make the bread herself. Whatever revelation she receives, that revelation must be obeyed, knowing in her heart that it will always be what she needs—nourishing and filling.

Now Is the Time to Act

One aspect of prayer that is often not considered is that with every prayer, there is an accompanying responsibility to respond—to act or perform as one is so guided. If a person is unwilling to accept that responsibility, then he is like the husband who asks his wife what he can do to be of help around the house, but grouses when she asks him to mop the kitchen floor and instead proceeds to go outside and mow the lawn. In all likelihood, a man's failure to act responsibly is more disappointing to God than it is to a spouse under comparable circumstances.

19. Boyd K. Packer, General Conference Report, "The Cloven Tongues of Fire," *Ensign,* May 2000, 8.

As an individual accepts the responsibility to act in accordance with the inspiration given, then let that person commit to act promptly like the prophet Alma. In attempting to preach the gospel to the people of Ammonihah, Alma "labored much in the spirit, wrestling with God in mighty prayer, that he would pour out his Spirit upon the people who were in the city." (Alma 8:10) Regrettably, the people of Ammonihah had hardened their hearts. As a consequence, Alma felt the need to call upon a more receptive community, so he departed toward the city of Aaron. While journeying to Aaron, an angel of the Lord appeared to Alma, directing him to return to Ammonihah to preach again to the people.

Did Alma say to the angel that he would return to Ammonihah when he got back from his vacation? Did he say he would get a man right on it? Did he say he would act after his favorite TV program was over? No, he acted promptly. Alma "returned speedily to the land of Ammonihah." (Alma 8:18)

When a man fails to act promptly, he may forever lose an opportunity to be of service to others or otherwise do the will of the Lord. One of my friends, David, learned this lesson. He had been praying for opportunities to recognize and act on the promptings of the Holy Ghost. While driving home from work one day, he saw several cars ahead of him swerving to avoid an object in the road. David did likewise. After passing the obstruction, he had the impression that he should stop, go back and remove the object from the road. David did not do what he was impressed to do, telling himself he was already past the object and was anxious to get home.

Then David recalled that he had been praying for such an opportunity to act as directed. Finally, he stopped and turned around. Just as he came upon the object from the opposite direction, he saw another car hit it, followed by a sudden trail of liquid streaming from under the car. David was disappointed in himself, because he had not acted promptly in accordance with the prompting he received. Had David acted on the first prompting, he may have been an answer to someone else's prayer, preventing a hardship or at least an inconvenience.

President Spencer W. Kimball used to tell church members to "do it" and to "do it now." President Kimball would have enjoyed working with the brother of Jared. The brother of Jared had been instructed by the Lord to get to work building a ship for his people. What did he do? He acted promptly. In the words of the scripture, he "did go to work." (Ether 2:16)

There is a simple test to determine whether or not a person has been moved by the Spirit. If the person does not act as guided, then the evidence shows that the Spirit has not moved that individual.

There are a few ways that a person can be moved by the Spirit. First, a man or woman can demonstrate that he or she is moved by physically saying or doing what the Spirit has directed should be said or done. Second, a person can show that he or she is moved by the Spirit by ceasing certain selfish or hurtful practices—the person can exercise restraint.

Third, a person may be moved by the Spirit by feeling a burning in one's breast, a lump in the throat or tears in one's eyes. To be moved by such a spirit, one will experience an increase of faith or desire to continue keeping the commandments as the person has been doing. If there is no increase of faith or recommitment to keeping the commandments, then the person probably was not moved by the Spirit, but experienced only a feeling of emotion.

When it comes time to act, people should choose wisely. The scriptures teach that there needs to be an opposition—such as good versus evil—in all things. Without that opposition, men and women cannot act for themselves. Therefore, in order to act, an individual needs to be influenced or enticed by either good or evil.[20] When answers to prayers are given, and one chooses not to follow the revelation provided, what spirit is it that guides that person to make such a poor choice? It must be an evil spirit. If a person keeps the commandments, prays properly and learns to recognize discernable answers when they come, that person will make the right choices and will know that it is by God that he or she is led.[21] With that knowledge one cannot be deceived.

When divine direction is given, when one desires to respond promptly as directed, there may be times when a person does not

20. 2 Nephi 2:15-16.
21. 1 Nephi 17:3; See also Alma 32:35.

feel like he has enough information to move ahead. At times like that there is a natural tendency to hesitate. In such instances, one should not stop moving, but rather get under way without delay. The hesitation to take action should not be a deterrent. The Spirit will continue to lead even though one may not know what to do next.[22] Everyone will be guided to know what to say and what to do.[23]

The mere simplicity of the Lord's counsel may also cause some to hesitate in doing what they feel prompted to do. The prompting may be so simple as to be downplayed into an idle thought rather than given the status of personal revelation that it deserves. For whatever reason, people often think that a prompting has to be grand and glorious to qualify as revelation. Such is not the case. All must treat the smallest of promptings and impressions with respect and gratitude.

This lesson that promptings of the Spirit do not need to be grand displays is taught in the Old Testament in 2 Kings, chapter 5. Naaman was a man who expected guidance from the Lord to be marvelous and impressive. But he learned otherwise. Naaman, a Syrian, was a captain—a great and mighty man. Unfortunately, he had contracted leprosy. It was made known to Naaman, by his wife's humble maid, that there was a prophet in Israel who could cure him of his leprosy. Arrangements were made for Naaman to visit Elisha the prophet. When Naaman arrived at the house of Elisha, he was neither formally greeted nor invited into the prophet's house. Instead, a messenger was sent to Naaman with instructions that he should wash himself in the Jordan River seven times and his leprosy would be healed.

One can understand how Naaman would be angry and hesitate to follow the advice of the prophet. Naaman was a great man, accustomed to grandeur and formality. In spite of his greatness, it was a modest maid who suggested he go to Israel. In addition, he was made to feel almost unwelcome at Elisha's house, and the counsel from the prophet was so nonsensical to him that he almost totally

---

22. 1 Nephi 4:6.
23. D&C 100:5; 2 Nephi 32:5.

dismissed it. Naaman had expected a wonderful miracle to occur under the hand of the prophet. In addition, Naaman could see no logical connection between the instructions given by the prophet and the cure he sought.

It was one of Naaman's humble servants who helped Naaman put the matter into perspective. The servant told Naaman that if the prophet had asked Naaman to do something great in order to be healed, he surely would have done it; consequently, if Naaman would do something great, would not Naaman also do this simple thing by washing in the river as counseled by the prophet? Whether out of humility or resignation, Naaman followed the advice of his servant, dipped himself in the river the requisite number of times and was healed.

The simple direction or counsel given by the Lord can lead to magnificent results. Everyone should act promptly upon the revelation provided in answer to prayers, no matter how simple such revelation may seem. Regarding such simple instructions, the Lord has said: "For behold, thus saith the Lord God: I will give unto the children of men line upon line, precept upon precept, here a little and there a little; and blessed are those who hearken unto my precepts, and lend an ear unto my counsel, for they shall learn wisdom; for unto him that receiveth I will give more; and from them that shall say, We have enough, from them shall be taken away even that which they have." (2 Nephi 28:30)

Record the Answer Given

There is good counsel from the scriptures with instruction for everyone to maintain a personal journal. This counsel is especially suited for one who receives answers to prayers: "For I command all men, both in the east and in the west, and in the north, and in the south, and in the islands of the sea, that they shall write the words which I speak unto them." (2 Nephi 29:11; See also Moses 1:40)

There is no difference between the scriptures as revealed through the prophets and the truths revealed to individuals through discernable answers to their prayers. Consequently, another responsibility that accompanies the prayer process is for everybody to record the divine impressions, words, feelings and other revelations given to them.

As one of the modern-day apostles suggested, "Write down impressions that come to mind as accurately as possible. This guidance is as real as the five senses. We often leave the most precious personal direction of the Spirit unheard because we do not record and respond to the first promptings that come to us when the Lord chooses to direct us or when impressions come in response to urgent prayer."[24] It takes courage and faith to record in a journal what one believes to be personal revelation. Yet as one does this, faith will grow and the person will learn line upon line, here a little, there a little, about both the personal revelation process and oneself.

---

24. Richard G. Scott, Church Educational System, Symposium, BYU, 1998.

9
He Answers

He Always Answers

Perhaps by merely reading this book one's attitude, practice and expectations about prayer have changed. Knowing that there is an answer to every single prayer must be one of the great reassuring blessings of mortal life. The current living prophet, Gordon B. Hinckley, confirms that, "The miracle of it all is that He hears. He responds. He answers—not always as we might wish He would answer, but there is no question in my mind that He answers."[1]

Mastering the ability to receive discernable answers to one's prayers is not a blessing granted only to men and women of the church serving in leadership capacities. It is a blessing available to every one and is something at which each person can succeed. We are promised by President Hinckley that, "We can be perfect in our prayers to our Father in Heaven. There are some things in which it is very difficult to be perfect, but I hope that everyone here, every man and woman and boy and girl, will get on his or her knees night and morning and thank the Lord for His blessings, thank the Lord for His kindness, thank the Lord for every gift that He has given, and pray for strength to do the right thing and remember before the Lord all who are in need and distress. We can be perfect in our prayers, my brothers and sisters."[2]

As we perfect our faith, adopt a more Christ-like character, prepare for prayer, include the key elements of a properly offered prayer, study the scriptural models of prayer and learn to recognize

---

1. Gordon B. Hinckley, "A Prophet's Counsel and Prayer for Youth," *Ensign,* Jan. 2001, 10.
2. Gordon B. Hinckley, "Inspirational Thoughts," *Ensign,* Jul. 1998, 2.

the different ways a discernable answer may be given, then one is ready to reap the benefits of the promises given: "If thou shalt ask, thou shalt receive revelation upon revelation, knowledge upon knowledge, that thou mayest know the mysteries and peaceable things."[3]

We have a Heavenly Father who loves us and answers each and every prayer. Likewise, we are also blessed to know that where much is given, much is expected. These blessings are real and the answers can be discernable.[4] We now have the responsibility to sanctify ourselves, because tomorrow, the Lord will do wonders among us.[5]

The Beginning

---

3. D&C 42:61; See also 1 Nephi 10:19; Enos 1:15; Moroni 9:21; Moroni 7:26; D&C 29:6; 88:64; John 14:13-14.
4. Alma 32:35.
5. Joshua 3:5.

Bibliography

Barton, Grant E. "On Bended Knee." *Ensign,* February 1996, 48.

Bassett, Arthur R. "Before Praying." *Ensign,* January 1976, 31.

Bennion, Francine. "Stone or Bread?" *Ensign,* January 1976, 38.

Bennion, Steven D. "Human Life Divided by Reason Leaves a Remainder," *Expressions of Faith: Testimonies of Latter-day Saint Scholars.* Salt Lake City: Deseret Book, 1996.

Benson, Ezra Taft. "Pray Always." *Ensign,* February 1990, 2.

Benson, Reed A. *The Teachings of Ezra Taft Benson.* Salt Lake City: Bookcraft, 1988.

Book of Mormon, The. An account written by the hand of Mormon upon plates taken from the plates of Nephi. Salt Lake City: The Church of Jesus Christ of Latter-day Saints, 1982.

Conference Report. Salt Lake City: The Church of Jesus Christ of Latter-day Saints, April 1964, 97.

Covey, Stephen R. and Sandra. "Teaching Our Children to Pray." *Ensign,* January 1976, 59.

Dahl, Larry E, and Cannon, Donald Q., eds. *Encyclopedia of Joseph Smith's Teachings.* Salt Lake City: Bookcraft, 1997.

Dahl, Larry E. "The Abrahamic Test." In *A Witness of Jesus Christ,* edited by Richard D. Draper. Salt Lake City: Deseret Book Company, 1990.

Doctrine and Covenants, The. Salt Lake City: The Church of Jesus Christ of Latter-day Saints, 1982.

Gibbons, Francis M. "The Dual Aspects of Prayer." General Conference Report. *Ensign,* November 1991, 78.

Groberg, John H. "The Lord's Wind." General Conference Report. *Ensign,* November 1993, 26.

Hickok, Eliza M. "Prayer." *Ensign,* February 1990, 5.

Hinckley, Gordon B. "A Prophet's Counsel and Prayer for Youth." *Ensign,* January 2001, 2.

——. "Inspirational Thoughts." *Ensign,* July 1998, 2.

History of the Church. Salt Lake City: Deseret Book Company, 1978. Seven volumes.

Hymns. "I Stand All Amazed." Salt Lake City: The Church of Jesus Christ of Latter-day Saints, no. 193.

——. "Lord, Accept Our True Devotion." Salt Lake City: The Church of Jesus Christ of Latter-day Saints, no. 107.

Jensen, Jay E. "Have I Received an Answer from the Spirit?" *Ensign,* April 1989, 21.

Juvenile Instructor. July 1873.

Kendrick, L. Lionel. "Personal Revelation." *Ensign,* September 1999, 7.

Kimball, Spencer W. *Faith Precedes the Miracle.* Salt Lake City: Deseret Book Company, 1972.

——. "Preparing for Service in the Church." General Conference Report. *Ensign,* May 1979, 47.

Leuders, Beth J. "Clarity." as quoted in *Reader's Digest,* November 2000, 24.

Maxwell, Neal A. "Insights." *New Era,* April 1978, 6.

McConkie, Bruce R. *Mormon Doctrine.* 2nd ed. Salt Lake City: Bookcraft, 1966.

——. "Why the Lord Ordained Prayer." *Ensign,* January 1976, 7.

Monson, Thomas S. "Goal Beyond Victory." General Conference Report. *Ensign,* November 1988, 44.

——. "The Path to Peace." General Conference Report. *Ensign,* May 1994, 60.

——. "Your Eternal Voyage." General Conference Report. *Ensign,* May 2000, 46.

Packer, Boyd K. "The Cloven Tongues of Fire." General Conference Report. *Ensign,* May 2000, 8.

——. "Personal Revelation: The Gift, the Test, and the Promise." General Conference Report. *Ensign,* November 1994, 59.

——. "Reverence Invites Revelation." General Conference Report. *Ensign,* November 1991, 21.

——. "The Candle of the Lord." *Ensign,* January 1983, 51.

Partridge, Thomas. "The Unexpected Answer." *Ensign,* February 2002, 37.

Pearl of Great Price, The. Salt Lake City: The Church of Jesus Christ of Latter-day Saints, 1982.

Pinegar, Rex D. "Peace Through Prayer." General Conference Report. *Ensign,* May 1993, 65.

Quotationary. CD, NovaSoft 1999.

Riddle, Chauncey C. "Obstacles to Prayer." *Ensign,* January 1976, 27.

Scott, Richard G. Church Educational System Symposium, BYU, 1998.

——. "Learning to Recognize Answers to Prayer." General Conference Report. *Ensign,* November 1989, 30.

——. "The Power of a Strong Testimony." General Conference Report. *Ensign,* November 2001, 87.

Talmage, James E. *Articles of Faith.* Salt Lake City: The Church of Jesus Christ of Latter-day Saints, 1947.

Tanner, N. Eldon. "Christ in America." General Conference Report. *Ensign,* May 1975, 34.

Taylor, Sally. "The Holy Ghost: Our Infallible Guide." *Speeches,* BYU Devotional Address, 5 November 1996.

Teaching, No Greater Call. Salt Lake City: The Church of Jesus Christ of Latter-day Saints, 1978.

Teachings of Presidents of the Church, Joseph F. Smith. Salt Lake City: The Church of Jesus Christ of Latter-day Saints, 1998.

Twain, Mark. "The Adventures of Huckleberry Finn." *The Portable Mark Twain,* New York: The Viking Press, 1968.

Welch, John W. "The Lord's Prayers." *Ensign,* January 1976, 15.

Index